Mapping Inner Space

Learning and Teaching **Mind Mapping**

By **Nancy Margulies, M.A.**

Zephyr Press

Mapping Inner Space

Grades K–Adult

©1991 Zephyr Press, Tucson, AZ
ISBN 0-913705-56-X

Illustrations: Nancy Margulies, M.A.
Editor: Kathryn Ring
Book Production: Richard Diffenderfer

Table of Contents

Foreword

Two years ago I received a phone call from a young woman in St. Louis requesting an appointment. She had heard about New Horizons for Learning, and she said she was eager to learn more about innovative educational strategies. She said she had some of her own!

The next week, Nancy Margulies walked into my Seattle office and introduced herself as a "mind mapper." Attractive, personable, and filled with boundless enthusiasm, she asked innumerable questions about learning and eagerly discussed new possibilities for education. She said she'd like to "hang around" for a few days, so I invited her to accompany me to a seminar I was giving for school personnel staff development the next morning.

As I was making my presentation, I noticed that Nancy was mind mapping a graphic record of the information. At the break, she went out to make photocopies for all the participants and, by the end of the morning, each person received a set of mind maps that summarized visually the entire presentation. That was the beginning of our happy association with Nancy. Since that memorable day she has developed strategies not only for mapping conferences and meetings, but for teaching the skill of mind mapping to others.

Nancy was a keynote presenter at the Education Summit at George Mason University, the New Horizons' Education Conference on Multiple Intelligences, and countless other teacher-education seminars. She has worked extensively with elementary-school students, bringing her creative touch to hundreds of children. She also worked for ten years as a psychologist in special education settings, focusing her work on deaf children, their parents, and teachers.

As our culture is catapulted into becoming a learning society, practical tools of learning must be made available to everyone. Nancy's strategies are not only practical, but tap into human resources that cannot be easily accessed through linear and more limited ways of thinking. Teachers and students alike can benefit from Nancy's approaches to mind mapping. The technique of mapping enhances our thinking skills, encourages cooperative learning, makes learning more fun and more memorable.

Mindscapes, Nancy's invention that goes beyond mind mapping, will lead you even further into the realm of intuitive and creative educational experiences.

Get ready for an adventure in learning and expect to discover some new talents with Nancy as your guide!

Dee Dickinson
President
New Horizons for Learning

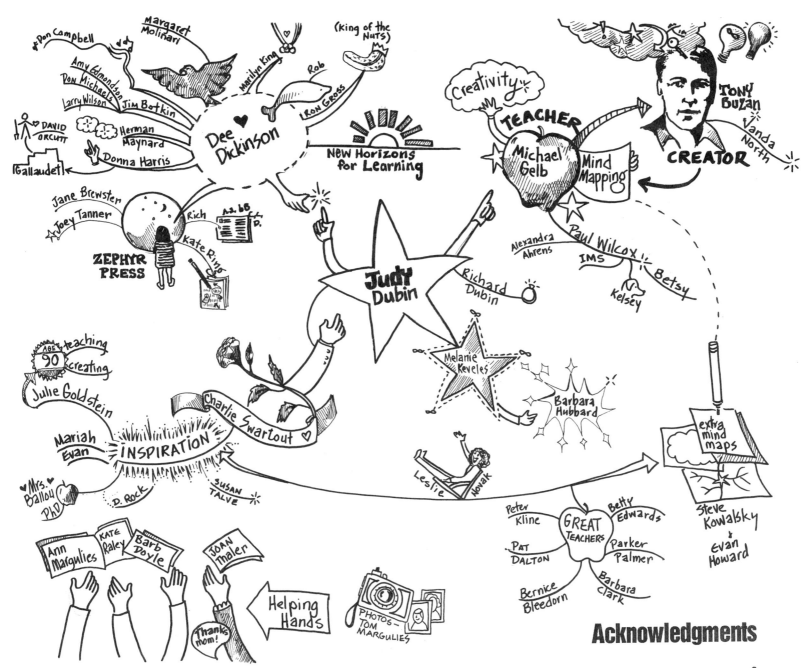

Don Campbell
Margaret Molinari
Amy Edmondson
Don Michaels
Larry Wilson
Jim Botkin
Marilyn King
Rob
(king of the Nuts)
Ron Gross
DAVID ORCUTT
Herman Maynard
Donna Harris
Gallaudet
Dee ♥ Dickinson
New Horizons for Learning

Jane Brewster
Joey Tanner
Rich
A-z 66
kate Ring
ZEPHYR PRESS

Creativity
TEACHER
Michael Gelb
Mind Mapping
TONY BUZAN
Vanda North
CREATOR

Alexandra Ahrens
Paul Wilcox
IMS
Betsy
Kelsey

Judy Dubin
Richard Dubin

teaching
AGE 90
creating
Julie Goldstein
Mariah
Evan
INSPIRATION
Charlie Swartout ♥
Mrs. Balloy PhD
D. Rock
SUSAN TALVE

Melanie Keveles
Barbara Hubbard

extra mind maps

Leslie Novak

Ann Margulies
KATE Raley
Barb Doyle
JOAN Thaler
Helping Hands
Thanks mom!
PHOTOS-TOM MARGULIES

Peter Kline
GREAT TEACHERS
Betty Edwards
Pat Dalton
Parker Palmer
Bernice Bleedorn
Barbara Clark

Steve Kowalsky & Evan Howard

Acknowledgments

3

Introduction

Mind mapping is a revolutionary system for pouring ideas onto paper. Through mapping, teachers and learners can enhance their thinking skills and become more freely creative. Using a central image, key words, colors, codes, and symbols, mind mapping is both fun and fast. It is rapidly replacing traditional note-taking and outlining in schools and workplaces throughout the world.

The process of mapping is very simple and can be introduced to anyone from five-year-olds to older adults. The trick in using mapping effectively is to practice the skill until it becomes automatic. For many of us, the traditional style of writing ideas in linear fashion, using one color on lined paper, is a deeply ingrained habit. Retraining the brain to draw ideas radiating from a central image takes practice and patience. However, once you have the basics of mapping, the obvious benefits will lead you to use this technique any time that you want to put ideas on paper.

This book is for everyone: teachers, students, parents, and children. It is based upon the principle that the best society is one in which education takes place everywhere, not just in schools. *Mapping Inner Space* is for the learner and teacher in each of us. For the teacher, the best approach to acquiring this new skill is first to learn it and then to teach it. After you have begun to map, you and your students can begin to create your own varieties and applications. Feel free to develop and share new ideas, forms, and applications. Think of mapping as a flexible, evolving system with unlimited potential — like the uncharted inner space of the human mind itself.

We have included a mind map for each page of text. In some cases the map will serve as an example of one of the uses of mapping; in other cases the map will contain all the information that is presented on the page opposite it. Usually, mind maps are created in color, and we have included some examples of color maps in this book. In most cases the maps are black and white. Some of the maps can be photocopied as handouts for your students. In other cases you may wish to add your own color to the maps by highlighting the elements that you want to emphasize or remember. You can also use colored felt-tip pens to add your own ideas to the maps.

Using Mind Mapping

Visual note-taking has been around for a long time. It is seen in the cave paintings of primitive man, in the hieroglyphics of ancient Egypt, and the notes and

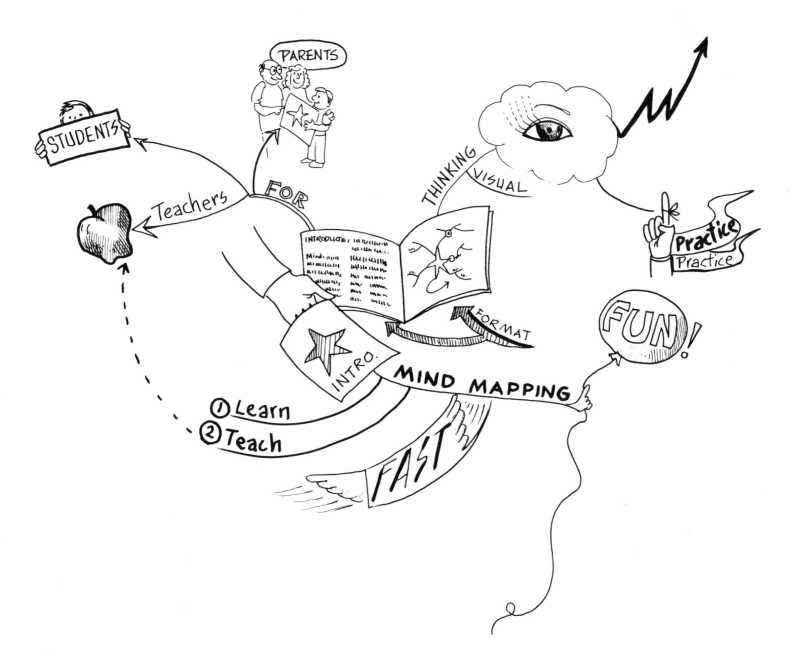

sketches of such great thinkers as Leonardo daVinci and Michelangelo. Left to their own devices, most children sketch and doodle while listening to new ideas. Before we establish language, we visualize pictures in our minds and link them to concepts. Unfortunately, we often block the creative channels by training children to write only words, monochromatically on lined paper. Now that educators are aware of the value of nurturing thinking skills and creativity, we can employ systems such as mind mapping that do not restrict, but rather, promote creative thinking.

You will notice that a mind map allows you to record a great deal of information on one page and to show relationships among various concepts and ideas. This visual representation helps you to think about a subject in a global fashion and lends to the flexibility of your thinking. On a map you can literally see the structure of the subject in a way that isn't possible with outlines. The variety of maps presented in this book is only a beginning. Once you learn to let your ideas and associations flow freely, you will no doubt create your own maps of uncharted territories.

Take a minute right now to recall the last time you had to prepare a lecture or paper. How easy was it to get started? How did the process flow? When creating an outline, one has to wait until the first idea, Roman Numeral One, has appeared. The next thought must follow in exact order and be a subset of Number One.

Of course, our brains don't work that way. We have numerous thoughts, images, mental pictures, and impressions occurring at the same time. Linear note-taking systems such as outlining simply can't keep up with our complexity of thought. Mind mapping does.

Many Applications

For teachers and parents mind mapping has some special applications. Aside from your own study, planning, and brainstorming, you can introduce your students or children to a study skill that will enable them to create an overview, take notes more efficiently, review for tests, and create visual records of their own ideas as well. I have found mapping extremely useful for presenting children with new ideas in context.

In mind mapping, many people can contribute their ideas to one map. For example, a family might plan a vacation together in the form of a map that includes the wishes and suggestions of each family member. In a classroom you can map any discussion, including negotiations, plans for a special project, or a group review of a topic you have just studied.

In addition, mind mapping is helpful to children who are deaf and use American Sign Language, which has no written component. Mind mapping provides these children with a means of recording ideas on paper, even though they are not fluent in written English. The language that is natural for children who sign is highly vi-

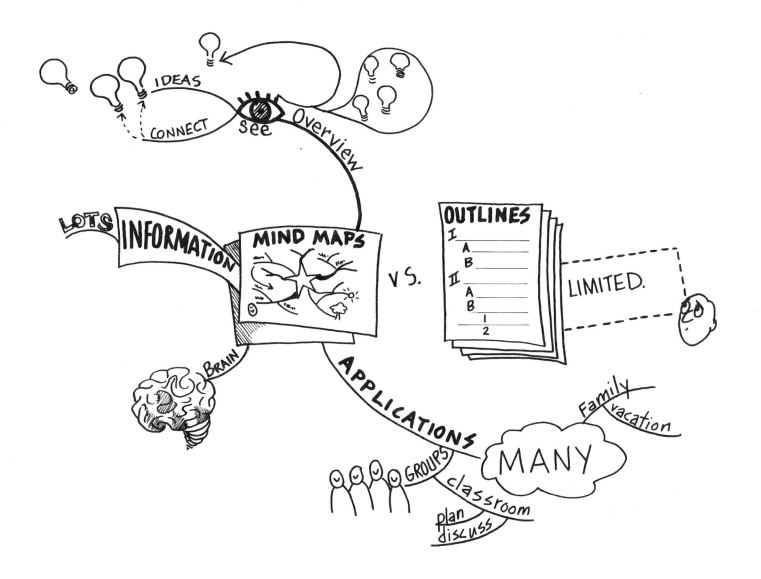

IDEAS
CONNECT
See
Overview

LOTS
INFORMATION
MIND MAPS
VS.
Brain

OUTLINES
I
  A
  B
II
  A
  B
    1
    2
LIMITED.

APPLICATIONS
GROUPS
plan
discuss
classroom
MANY
Family
vacation

7

sual and conceptual — so is mind mapping.

Mapping is also extremely useful for dyslexic children and "nontraditional learners" who may be labeled learning disabled. In fact, many children find a nonlinear approach much more natural for expressing their ideas. When encouraged to map their thoughts, these children are allowed a fuller range of expression.

To help you get started in sketching your own symbols for mind mapping, step-by-step instructions have been included to take you through the creation of a number of simple drawings. Many of the pages can be used as handouts for students as they practice their symbol-drawing abilities.

Mindscapes

The final segment of this book introduces a note-taking form that goes beyond the rules of mind mapping and enables you to represent your ideas graphically, in any form that suits your needs. This system I call "Mindscaping." Mindscapes do not necessarily have a central image but can begin anywhere on the page and incorporate words, phrases, quotations, cut-out images from magazines, or anything else that you might decide to use. Mindscapes are easier to develop after you have practiced and become more comfortable with the basics of mind mapping.

Now *you* have an opportunity to develop a personal style as a mind mapper and to join your students or family in discovering new applications for this remarkable system.

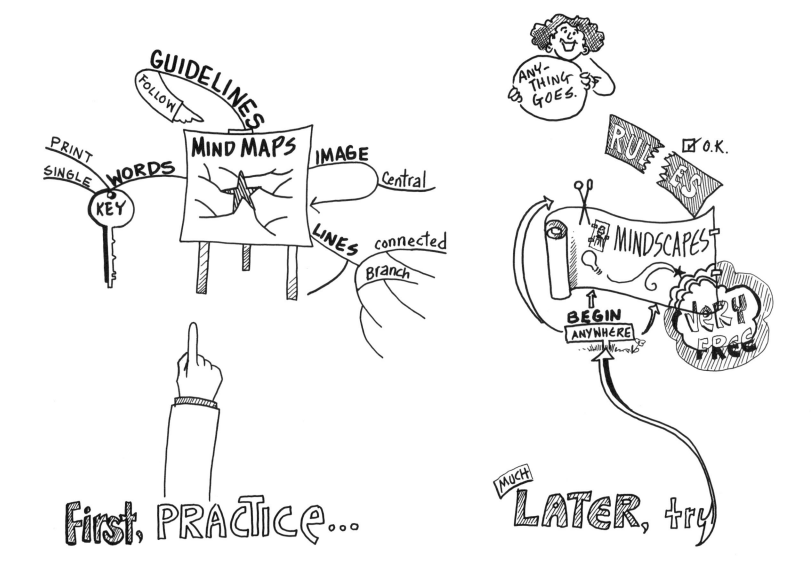

GUIDELINES

Follow

MIND MAPS

PRINT
SINGLE
WORDS
KEY

IMAGE
Central

LINES
connected
Branch

First, PRACTICE...

ANY-
THING
GOES.

RULES
☑ O.K.

MINDSCAPES

BEGIN
ANYWHERE

VERY
FREE

MUCH LATER, try

9

Overview

The world in which we live is changing rapidly and radically. Education has to take on a whole new meaning. The skills that we must nurture and develop today are utterly different from those needed in the past. Not long ago education was a process that ended at high school for most people. The primary goal was preparation for work. Today education is best described as a process, ongoing, lifelong, and provided not only in schools, but in the workplace and community as well.

One of the most reassuring aspects of the challenge to educators is that we already have a wealth of powerful information about how to teach in dynamic, multisensory, accelerated styles that can bring out the best in each individual learner. In the bibliography, I have included a list of books and publications that clearly define these educational techniques. This book addresses one approach that can be integrated with each of the others.

Before our modern information era, one of the tasks assigned to all students was to memorize facts and repeat them when called upon. The emphasis was almost exclusively on content. Now, in the age of the computer, there is no need to become a storehouse for facts and dates. Computers can do a much more efficient job of information storage and retrieval. The challenge now is to do well what the computers cannot do. We must develop our abilities to use the information available with creativity, intuition, and human ingenuity. Each of us must be able to work well both individually and with others in synergistic exchanges.

One of the primary reasons that we are now better equipped to update our styles of education is that we have increasing amounts of information about the workings of the human brain. More than 90 percent of what we now know about the human brain is the result of research conducted in the last ten years!

In the early 1970s, Dr. Roger Sperry at the University of California discovered that the two lobes of our cerebral cortex function very differently. The right side is more active when we are engaged in nonverbal activities, such as relaxing while listening to music, drawing, and daydreaming. The left side is active when we are using language, solving math problems, and processing data in a linear, sequential manner.

Although in recent years Sperry's original premise has been greatly modified, the analogy is still useful. Our traditional methods of recording ideas encourage us to move from one idea to the next in a strictly linear, sequential, "left-brained" fashion. Note-taking of this sort limits our ability to see the big picture and make new connections among the ideas we are recording.

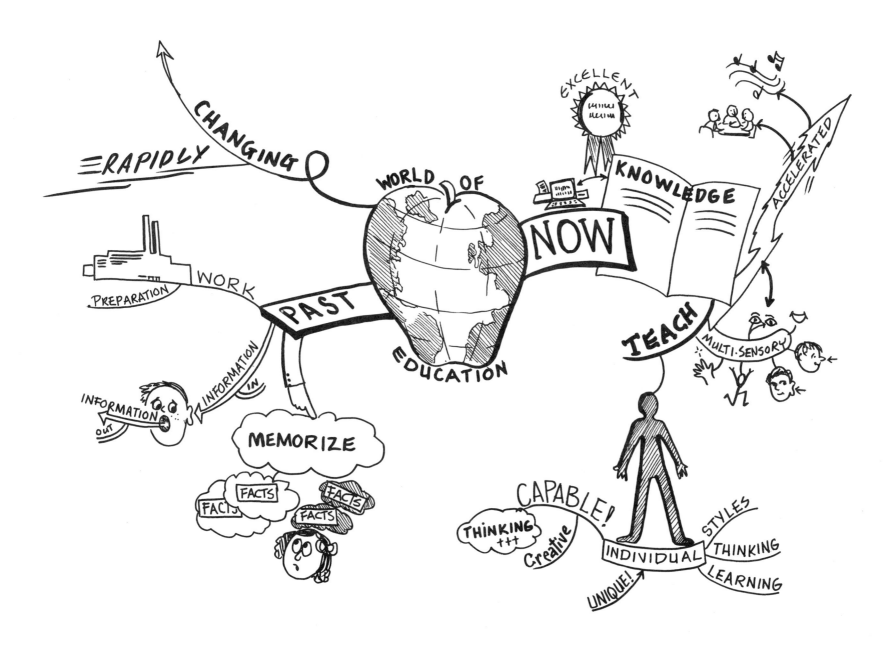

11

After studying the research of Sperry and his colleagues, Tony Buzan developed mind mapping. Buzan's system is designed to integrate the processing styles of the left and right hemispheres. When mapping, one is challenged to record ideas using not only words, but also symbols. In order to create a symbol one must use whole brain processing — words and images. Michael Gelb, an American lecturer and author, further developed the system of teaching mapping and pioneered the development of mind mapping as a tool for developing thinking skills.

The system was well received by educators and businesspeople in Europe who found that using mind maps enabled them to develop a far greater number of creative ideas than any of the traditional forms such as list making and outlining. Everyone can benefit from advancing thinking skills and becoming an expert at mapping the workings and understandings of his or her own mind.

In the twenty years since Tony Buzan invented mind mapping there has been increasing evidence that the ability to put thoughts into images as well as words enhances thinking skills and actually improves intelligence. It appears that the benefits of mind mapping extend far beyond the practical application of recording ideas to the realm of higher-order thinking and increased intelligence. (Wenger 1990)

Norman Cousins, in his excellent book on the power of the mind in healing entitled *Head First — The Biology of Hope*, describes the brain: *"Not even the universe, with its countless billions of galaxies, represents greater wonder or complexity than the human brain. The human brain is a mirror to infinity. There is no limit to its range, scope, or capacity for creative growth. It makes possible new perceptions and new perspectives, just as it clears the way for brighter prospects in human affairs."* (Cousins 1989, 71)

The illustration on page 13 represents the processing styles of the left and right hemispheres of the human brain.

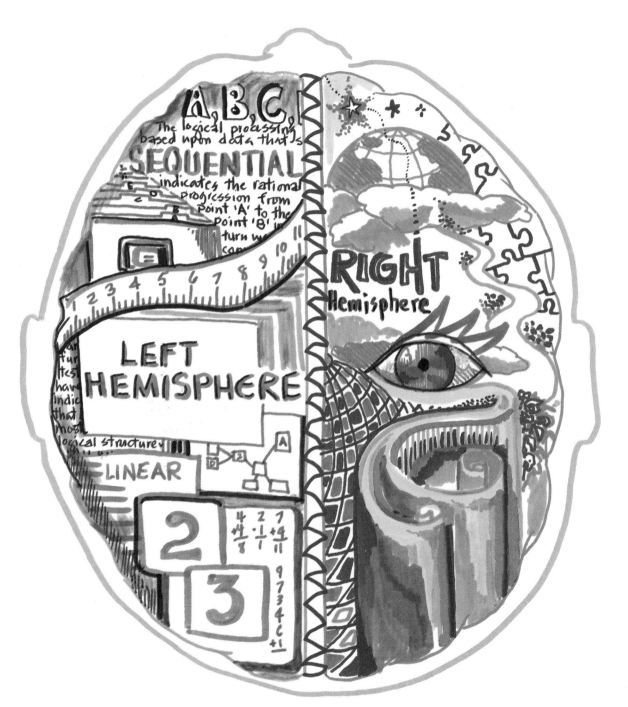

Chapter 1

Becoming a Mind Mapper

Remember the last time you attended a workshop or seminar? Do you remember the experience of taking notes? More importantly, do you remember reading your notes later to recall the lecture? Most people report that note-taking is frustrating, and many have so much trouble reading their own handwriting that they never bother to refer to the notes again. What about writing a paper or preparing a speech? Does the mere thought of it give you shivers and an overwhelming urge to clean your garage first?

Mind mapping creates notes that are easy to read and very fast to produce. As you will see, thoughts are pared down to essential key words, and many concepts are presented in a single symbol. Once you get the hang of it, you will find that getting started is no trouble — it's child's play.

Of course, before you teach mapping, you need to learn to make your own maps.

Materials you will need:
  unlined paper, 11" x 17" or larger
  medium felt-tip markers in a variety of colors
  several broad-tip pastel markers for highlighting

The easiest way to start mapping is to record your own ideas and to generate new ideas in the process. This form of individual brainstorming will give you an immediate experience of the power of mind mapping. In order to do that, set aside a thirty-minute period of time, find a comfortable, well-lit place to work, and think of a topic. Topics that work well for this first personal mind mapping include:

▶ plans for the day

▶ plans for the week

▶ goals for the year (or the next five, ten, twenty years)

▶ memories of a specific event

▶ strategies for a new project

▶ a map about your interests and hobbies

▶ the highlights of a book you read recently

COLORS

HIGHLIGHTERS

Pens

MATERIALS

PAPER

7"

11"

LARGE

LARGER!

UNLINED

OWN

IDEAS RECORD

GENERATE

many

My First Map

TIME 30 MIN. unhurried

Memories

TOPICS

INTERESTS

Comfortable

LIGHTING GOOD

SETTING

DAY

WEEK

PLANS

1

5

10

YEAR

FUTURE

GOALS

15

The First Phase: Generating

This phase of mind mapping, recording all ideas that occur to you, can be thought of as personal brainstorming.

■ Once the topic is selected, draw a picture or symbol that represents the topic. Place the image in the center of the paper and keep it fairly small so that there is still plenty of room left for the ideas you will be recording. (Notice the size of the central image in the maps in this book.) When you draw a symbol and wonder if you will be able to remember later what it represents, write a word or two next to the picture.

■ After you have drawn a central image, let your mind freely move to any association to your topic. Use several colors and add dimension if possible. Remember that this map is for you. The drawings should help you remember your topic, but they don't have to be great works of art.

■ Use key words in your mapping. Although it is sometimes difficult, try to put no more than one word on a line. This will assist you in developing the habit of paring down your notes to the truly essential elements. Beyond that, when you put only one word on a line, you can easily branch out, adding other words that you associate with the first word. From those words you may generate more words until you have branched out in many directions from the initial image. The words that

you select will be ones that convey the most information. Obviously, words such as "of, the, it," and, "an," are not key words (unless you are mapping a plot for "The Day IT Ate Cleveland").

Symbols that come to your mind as you generate ideas can be used either with key words or instead of them. Many people have trouble thinking of images at first or worry that they can't draw well enough. I advise students to make a quick sketch of a symbol idea, or leave a space so that they can return later to draw a symbol. As a practiced mind mapper, I have found that it is often faster for me to draw an image than it is to write the word.

Keep in mind that symbols can be developed for concepts, not only as substitutes for single words. (If you are absolutely stuck and can't think of a symbol for your central image, just draw a shape or cloud in the center and return to that space later to create an image.) After practicing mind mapping and reading the chapter on symbols, you will find that drawing symbols comes more easily. A drawn image is highly memorable and can call to mind a wealth of associations. That is one of the reasons it is best to stick with as many symbols as possible.

■ If you are making a map about your summer plans, you might have a sun and a sailboat as your central image, like the one on page 17.

■ Your first association might be that you plan to attend

LEARN

a course in sailing. For that association one key word should be selected, such as COURSE or CLASS or LEARN. You might use an arrow to point to the sailboat and an apple to represent learning.

■ Next, your mind might jump to your plan to drive to Denver to visit your mother during the summer. A symbol of a car and an arrow pointing to MOM is one way to record the idea. Remember, there is no one way to record any idea, no single image or word that should be used for a specific idea. Use what appeals to you, and soon you will find that you have a range of symbols available.

As you continue this early phase of mapping, let your mind relax and continue to record any thoughts that occur to you. Allow your creative and intuitive abilities to come out. Later there will be opportunities to edit and refine, if necessary.

As ideas occur to you, try not to judge them but rather to "allow" them. No idea is too outrageous to be put on the map. You may find that the most bizarre idea is often the one that leads to a creative breakthrough.

■ For example, if while drawing the image of driving to Denver, you think of John Denver singing in an outdoor concert, put that on the map, too. You might draw a few musical notes, a moon, and people on blankets, or if that seems too tricky, leave out the people and let it go with a sign that says "Concert Tonight" with musical notes surrounding it.

■ That seemingly silly thought might lead you to plan your trip to coincide with a concert of one of your favorite singers — perhaps John Denver himself.

(If you have a totally unrelated thought, such as "Oh, no, I forgot to call Sue," don't map that, but rather place it in a note in a corner of the map, like the one on the opposite page. I like to make notes to myself in the same place on each map, so that I can later skim the maps and see what unrelated items occurred to me that I need to put on my "to do" map.)

Using one key word on each line is important. Although there are times when you need to use a few words (such as a specific name), most often you can convey the thought with one word per line. One of the advantages of this guideline is that it allows you to attach other words to the key word as you make multiple associations to it. When you think of the idea of "driving to Denver to visit Mother" and write the words "Driving to Denver to Visit Mother," associating each aspect of the thought would be difficult. But, when you write just one word, DENVER, other activities you might do while in Denver may occur to you.

Or the associations to DRIVE might be a record of other places you might drive to, other people who might drive with you, or repairs you might need to have made to your car before driving.

One word per line is useful for developing a new habit: that of writing only the essential information on the page and eliminating extraneous data. You can imagine how handy this is when taking notes in a lecture. We tend to write down much more than we really need and usually don't take the time to go through our notes later. With practice you will be able to single out the key words and images you need to produce excellent notes quickly .

Maps offer you an opportunity to add emphasis to words through color, size, shape, and symbols. When a word is important, record it so that it jumps out and grabs your attention. The emphasizing of words not only brings attention to the more important aspects of the map but also keeps you in a creative mode as you discover new and unusual ways to emphasize. Our memories are greatly assisted in this process because anything that is unusual is much more memorable. So use emphasis for words and concepts that you want to remember. The mind map on the opposite page is a sample of the map that might be created from the topic "summer plans."

Review

After you have freely associated to your topic and recorded your ideas in key words and symbols, you can stop to take a look at the map thus far. You have completed the first phase of mind mapping at this point, the pouring of ideas onto paper. As you review your map,

you can add any new thoughts that occur to you.

When you need more space, there are several things you can do.

■ If you have room elsewhere on the map to continue a thought, just use a line or arrow to a new place and continue mapping. To do this, you need only to be willing to move beyond our traditional notions about writing everything in a neat, sequential order.

■ You can also take an idea that you want to expand and make it the center of a new map. Often this happens when brainstorming and planning new projects.

■ A third option is to tape your map to a larger sheet of paper and continue expanding the map.

The Second Phase: Organizing

In this phase you will organize and add codes and symbols to the map as needed. For example, suppose you created a map of all your ideas regarding the trip to Denver. You might then want to add a code or highlight to indicate all the things you need to do to prepare for the trip. You also could add arrows to connect certain elements of the map.

New Ideas — New Map

In some cases you may redraw the entire map and add a new order to it. The Denver trip could be redrawn to group all the preparations in one area and then show

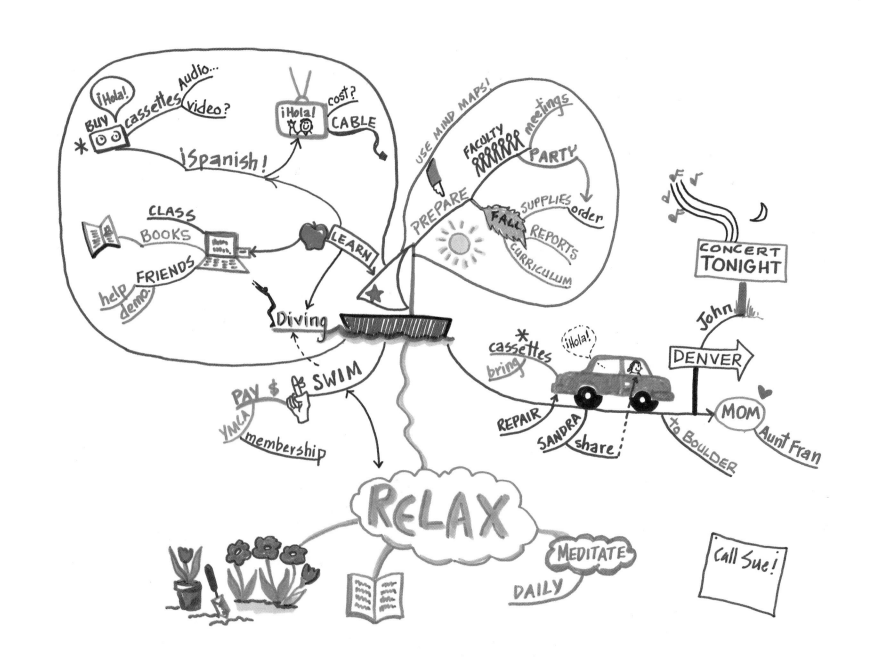

each day of the trip.

Sometimes, after creating your initial map, it is helpful to post the map where you can see it, think about it, and add new ideas that occur to you over a period of several days. You may then decide to redraw the map to include only the best ideas.

■ To accomplish this, use a highlighter or code to mark the best ideas on your original map. Draw a line around each distinct branch of the map to define specific sections.

Feel free to cross out ideas you don't want to keep and to add arrows to show relationships. It's fine if the map becomes messy. The old rule of neat, orderly papers doesn't apply here. In fact, the goal is to generate your ideas freely without limiting yourself.

When you are ready to draw a new map, you can create one that is clear and more orderly.

■ Try using a clock as the basis of organization. Draw your first line toward the one o'clock position and proceed in a clockwise order. Now you have a map that is very easy to read.

Mapping a Book

One of the best uses of mapping for study can be applied by anyone who needs to read a book for information. This idea, like mind mapping itself, is the creation of Tony Buzan.

Before you read a book, make a mind map of it. To perform this astounding feat:

■ Skim the book looking at the table of contents, foreword, introductions, summaries, charts, illustrations, and index. The index, where each topic is listed with page numbers, can net some valuable information. Any listing that occurs on many pages is probably a key element in the book.

■ After a quick perusal, make a large skeleton map that covers the key topics of the book. This might be as simple as the chapter headings but could be any system that gives you an overview of the book. From this beginning you will gain a sense of the book's content.

Ron Gross, a noted educator and author, states in his audiotape, *Peak Learning*, that we need to learn to read not faster, but smarter. He is referring to the fact that there is so much to read and such an abundance of information available that one can no longer expect to read every book from cover to cover. Instead, a reader can gain an overview of a book by skimming it, and then decide whether or not to read it or what parts to read.

■ When I read a book for information, I create a skeleton map that I then fold and keep in the front of the book.

■ For books on which I will take lots of notes I use Post-it notes to copy key phrases and page references as I read. Before writing, I turn the Post-its upside down

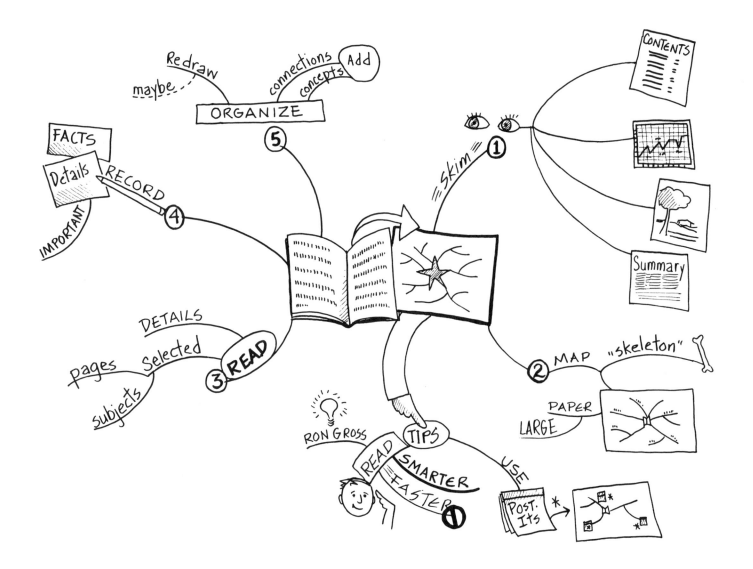

Redraw
maybe
ORGANIZE
connections   concepts   Add
⑤

CONTENTS

FACTS
Details   RECORD
IMPORTANT
④

=Skim= ①
👁 👁

Summary

DETAILS
pages   Selected
③ READ
subjects

② MAP   "skeleton" 🦴

PAPER
LARGE

RON GROSS
READ SMARTER FASTER 🚫

TIPS

USE
POST.
Its

💡

so that they can be positioned to stick up over the top of the pages like bookmarks.

■ After reading a chapter I place the Post-its on the larger map or copy them onto the map. I often record the related page number so that I can return to read more detail as needed.

■ If I want to imprint the ideas more fully in my memory, I redraw the map, organizing it to reflect the major concepts and their relationship to each other. By the time this task is completed, I not only have clear notes, but also I have presented my individual way of seeing the structure of the book. When I want to review or refer to the material in that book, the map serves as an excellent reference.

Preparing a Talk

Suppose that you are going to talk to your faculty about the key points of cooperative learning.

■ You might begin with a central image of three students working together under a banner that says CO-OPERATIVE LEARNING. The images turn out to look like primitive stick figures, but you are a daring soul and remind yourself that you don't need sophisticated renderings for a mind map. Radiating from the central image you might then add key words such as SKILLS, CHALLENGES, USES, AGE GROUPS, and BENEFITS. From these you associate to many more thoughts about

cooperative learning and think of an example or two from your own classroom.

■ After recording all these thoughts, stop to review. The map seems complete and completely messy. Now, in the organization phase you have a chance to clean up your act by redrawing the map. You may wish to add numbers to your messy first map to indicate the order in which you will redraw the parts. You could number the items to correspond with the order in which you will present them to your colleagues. Begin the second map with a central image and the first point in the one o'clock position. As you move clockwise around the central image, add each point.

■ For a lengthy presentation you may wish to draw two maps. (I find it easiest to record only the key words and images that will trigger my memory about each aspect of the topic, allowing me to map the entire presentation on one page.)

This technique is particularly useful when you are planning to present your ideas to others. You can glance at the map and see each idea in order. If you are giving a lecture, a map that has been drawn in order is easy to follow. The entire lecture can be on one map.

Shortening Your Talk

If you are running short on time, you can look at the map, see all the topics you are planning to cover,

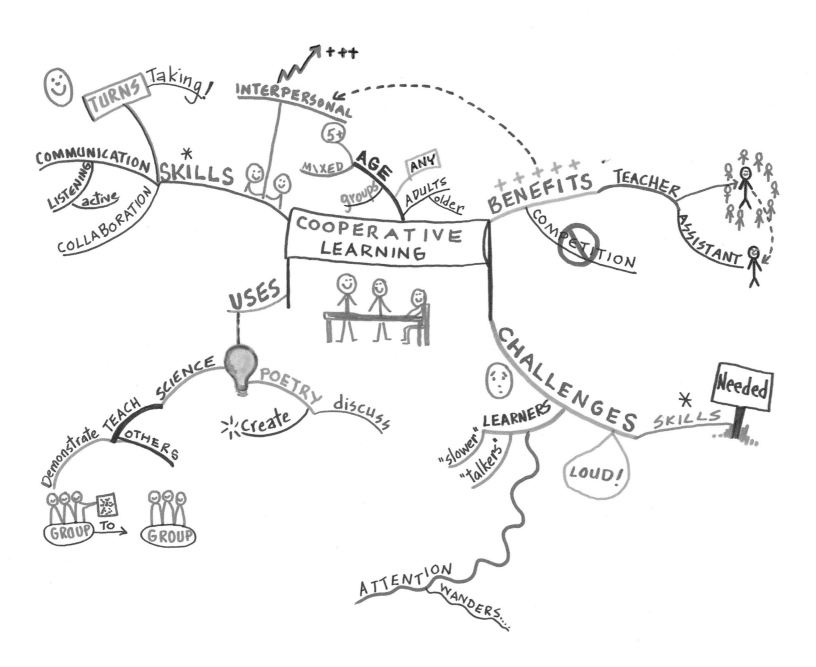

TURNS Taking!

INTERPERSONAL +++

COMMUNICATION

LISTENING active

COLLABORATION

SKILLS *

5+

MIXED groups AGE ANY ADULTS older

COOPERATIVE LEARNING

BENEFITS

COMPETITION

TEACHER ASSISTANT

USES

Demonstrate TEACH SCIENCE OTHERS

Create POETRY discuss

GROUP TO GROUP

CHALLENGES

"slower" LEARNERS "talkers"

LOUD!

SKILLS *

Needed

ATTENTION WANDERS...

and decide what to abbreviate or eliminate.

When your map is redrawn in an organized fashion, leaving out all extraneous material and adding any useful codes or symbols, you have a map that you can read clearly years later and that you are more likely to remember. One of the great benefits of mind mapping is that maps are so highly memorable — especially the ones that you create and redraw.

Visuals

You may decide that the map would make a good visual aspect of your presentation. In that case you could draw the map on poster board and show it to the group.

■ The map could then serve as a tool for previewing what you are going to discuss as well as reviewing at the end of the presentation.

■ You might even give everyone a small photocopy of the map or leave your poster board map on display to encourage others to review the material.

■ You could leave a large map in the faculty room with key points and lots of space left open for other teachers to add their own ideas. As you can see, the creative applications are abundant.

(Using mind mapping for presentations is explained in great detail by Michael Gelb in his book *Present Yourself.* If you give presentations regularly, Gelb's book will be extremely useful.)

Time Management

Mind mapping is an excellent tool for planning your day, week, month, and future goals. Before creating maps for daily plans, it is valuable to look at the larger picture.

The Overview

Take time to make a map for yourself on the topic of MY VALUES AND PRINCIPLES. On this map include everything that is important in your life. It may be helpful to answer the following questions:

▶ What is most important to me?

▶ Who is most important?

▶ What would I like to have more or less of in my life?

▶ What is my larger purpose in life?

Your answers to these questions may change from time to time, but generally, when you look at your life from this broad perspective, you will find that your basic values and principles are constant. The trick is to live your life is such a way that your actions are in keeping with your values.

One way to accomplish this is to plan your days to allow time for that which you really value. Most of us can identify with the busy professional who has so much to do and so many demands on his or her schedule that children and family, friends, and social concerns get short

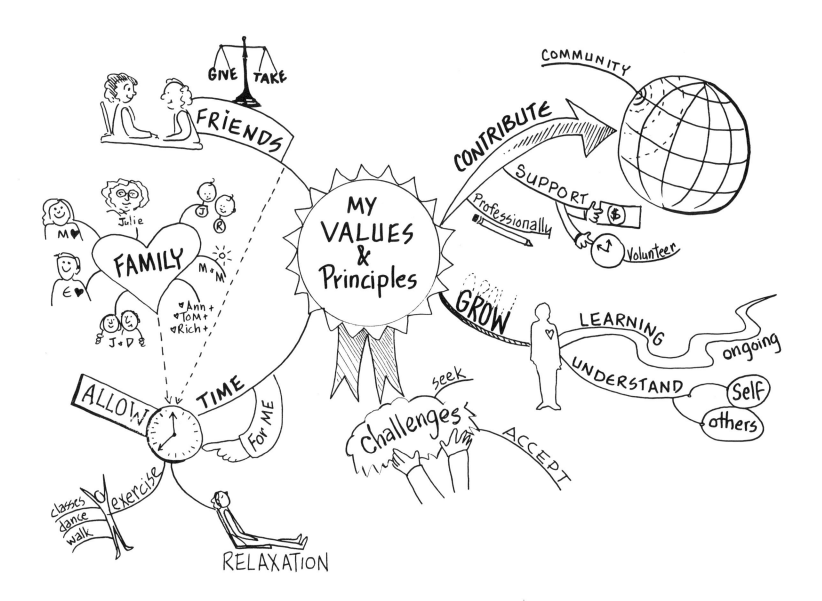

GIVE TAKE

FRIENDS

COMMUNITY

CONTRIBUTE

SUPPORT

Professionally

$ Volunteer

MY VALUES & Principles

FAMILY

Julie

J R

M ♥

M ♥ M

Ann + Tom + Rich +

J + D

GROW

LEARNING

ongoing

UNDERSTAND

Self

others

ALLOW

TIME

For ME

seek

Challenges

ACCEPT

classes dance walk exercise

RELAXATION

27

shrift. It is easy for this to happen, but it is possible to make a change.

Mapping Yourself

Before planning the specifics of a week or day, look at your life, not only in terms of values, but in terms of the roles that you play. Make another map with a symbol representing YOU in the center. Radiating from this image, create symbols for each important role that you play. Mine include MOTHER, FRIEND, WRITER, CONSULTANT, DAUGHTER, CITIZEN, and ARTIST. Include a role that represents your responsibilities to your SELF, too. When planning my time, I keep each of these roles in mind, making certain that none are lost and forgotten in the rush of daily activities.

Weekly Plan

A system that works extremely well for weekly planning involves taking an overview look at how you spend your time. This system is based upon the advice of Stephen Covey, an author and corporate trainer who has assisted thousands of executives to be more efficient and effective in their work and personal lives. For most of us, there are areas of our lives or tasks that we intend to do but never seem to get around to. To create a better balance of time use, take a look at these categories:

URGENT AND IMPORTANT (UI):
Those things that must be done immediately.

NOT URGENT BUT IMPORTANT (NU-I):
This category needs special attention. The activities that fall into this area include exercise, relaxation time, time with family or friends, reading that you enjoy, letters that you want to write, and so on.

URGENT BUT NOT IMPORTANT (U-NI):
In this category are the activities that someone else tells you must be done immediately or that you find yourself rushing to accomplish without first deciding how important they really are. If your supervisor calls and says that you must do something immediately, you might ask, "How urgent is this?" or "Please explain the importance of this."

NOT IMPORTANT AND NOT URGENT (NI-NU):
These activities can be postponed or planned for a later date. They should not be put ahead of the other categories. (Covey 1989)

Making Your Map

On Sunday evenings or the first thing Monday morning, I take time to plan the week. The map that I

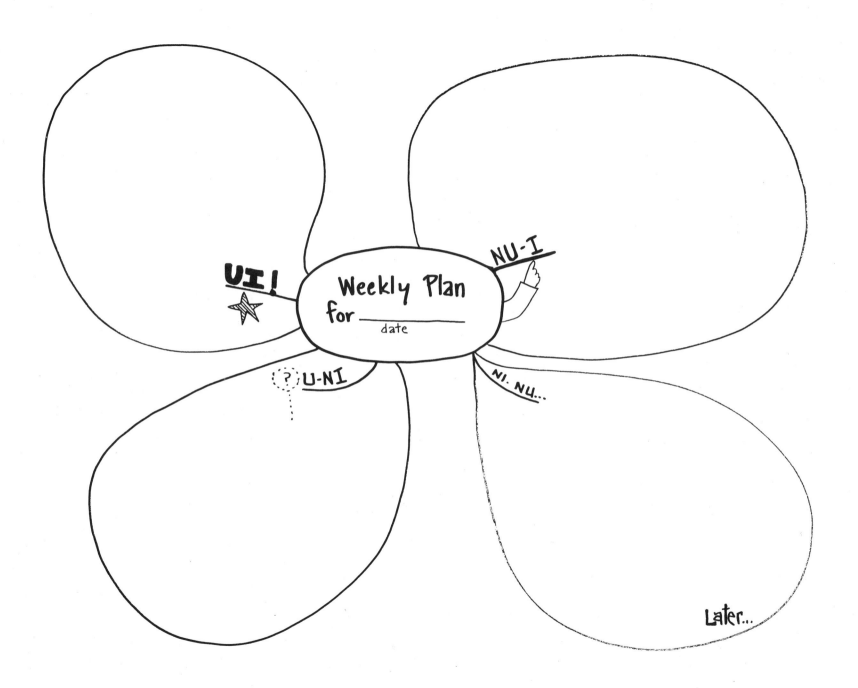

create on page 29 is divided into four quadrants. I look at the first one, Urgent and Important (UI), in order to plan exactly when I will take care of these items. Each UI item is scheduled into the week, at the earliest possible time. When I receive a call or request that is UI, I write it in the first quadrant where it will not escape my attention.

■ Next I look at Not Urgent but Important (NU-I) and make sure that I have scheduled these areas into my week. In NU-I, I include time with my children, exercise, and reading. These each receive a specific time and day. If urgent matters take precedence over one of these areas during the week, they are scheduled into the following week and highlighted.

■ I look at my roles map, too, making certain that I have provided time for each in my week. A symbol that represents my SELF appears in each week's plan. This might take the form of time to be alone and quiet, time to take a long walk, time to read a novel, and so on. For me, making time for SELF activities is the toughest, but the result is that I am much more effective in my other roles.

Daily Plan

You can create a daily plan with the four categories as well, or use any calendar that suits your schedule. If you need to make hourly appointments, then a planner with every hour accounted for is necessary.

Using my weekly plan as a source, I create daily plans each morning.

■ I begin with a simple symbol representing the day ahead and then create branches for topics such as phone calls, errands, projects, and correspondence. Calls that need to be made in the evening are represented by a phone receiver and a moon and errands by a car. The value of a map in planning a day is that you can group activities any way that serves you best and can then add to the map by category.

■ If I receive a phone call and need to add a new activity to the map, I either write it directly on the map or on a Post-it note that can be affixed to the map. The Post-its are handy because you can write the notes and then decide where to place them on the map. If you don't complete the task on one day, move the Post-it to the map for the next day.

Book of Maps

My planning maps are in a tablet that I have made at the local copy center. I purchase 50 sheets of 11" x 17" paper and have them spiral bound. I keep this book open on my desk for handy reference. If I need to look back at information from a previous day, it's convenient to do so. If I remember some errand that I need to do later in the day, I can write it with the other tasks related to the "car" branch. When I am ready to leave

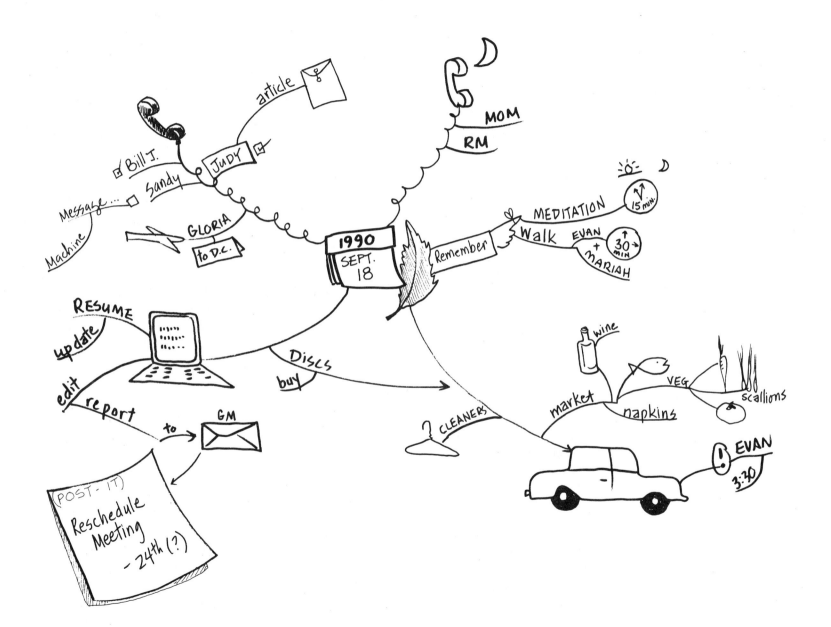

my office, it is easy to look at the map and see all the errands in one area. With list making that isn't possible.

One of the beauties of mind mapping is that it fosters individuality and creativity. No two maps look alike, and the design for your time management can be whatever suits you best. The samples on page 33 give you an idea of a couple of ways that a daily plan can be developed.

Reviewing Your Day

Maps can be used to review your day as well. Here is a suggestion from Peter Kline's *Everyday Genius:*

> "...*try mind mapping how you spent your time today. Now look at the whole picture of the day and think about other configurations that might have been possible, and perhaps more satisfying. What useless actions might have been eliminated? What enjoyable activities might get a little more time? You'll soon appreciate how the mind map gives you a global view of a time period, enabling you to make judgements that linear outline would only obscure from your thinking.*
>
> *One of the difficulties I have with scheduling my day in sequence is that it doesn't allow me to do things in the order in which I desire to do them as I proceed through time. A mind map, by not forcing me into a particular sequence, allows my activities to develop organically, yet I always know*

> *how what I'm doing fits in with the rest of what I plan to do." (Kline 1988, 248)*

Another review method for looking at your day is a visual record called "Charting the Day." Kaye Hayes, a master teacher and one of the innovators of Imaginal Education, reports that she has used and taught this technique with great success for many years:

- Place a paper in front of you horizontally and then draw a line across the length of it.

- Mark hourly time intervals from left to right.

- Next record ten or more events and the approximate times they occurred.

- Then look at your day and decide upon the most significant event of the day or the event which was pivotal. Place a star above it.

- Create titles for the times before and after the starred event.

- Next give a title to the day. This process is simple and very fast, yet if you make it a habit, you will soon have a journal that records the memorable events of every day.

(Samples, "Experiencing Your Experience" 1989)

Introducing Units in Curriculum

Maps can provide an effective preview of what will be covered in a unit. This same map can be posted as an overview and later used as a review.

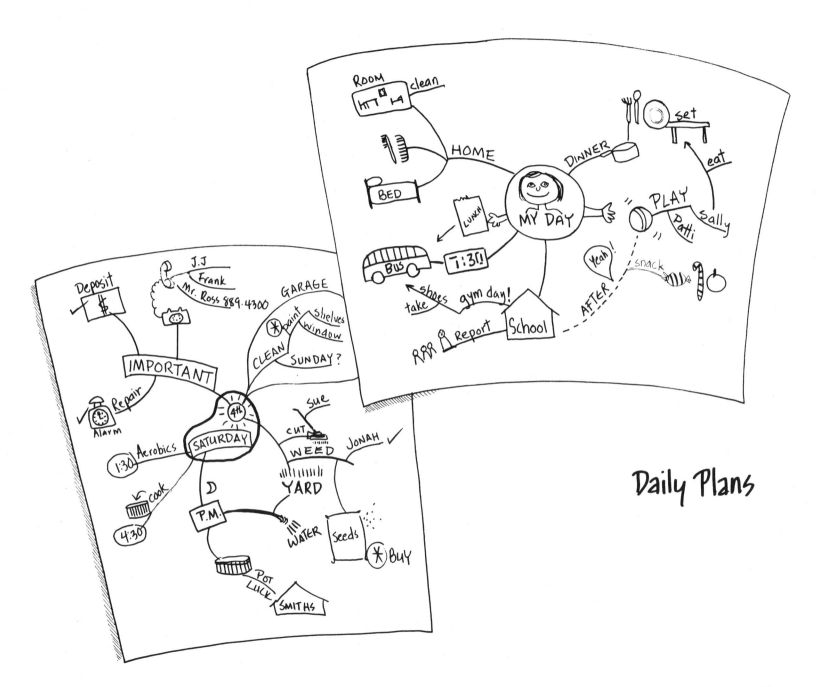

Daily Plans

■ To introduce a unit, make a map large enough to allow your class can see the entire plan. As you explain what will be covered, the class can follow along on the map.

■ As you teach the unit, you can add additional information. For example, you could list reading assignments in one color, positioning each assignment where it relates to the topics to be covered.

■ You could expand the map to include information about skills the students will be developing and how this information can be applied in other aspects of life. As you can see, the creative applications are abundant.

■ The map that you create could also be mural-size, drawn on a roll of butcher paper and taped to a wall.

■ During the time you are studying the subject, students add their own ideas and information to the map. For example, you could present the basic elements of a unit on the Civil War and ask students to add to the map the details of battles, political decisions, cultural differences between the North and South, and impact on black Americans.

■ Instead of drawing directly on the map, you might distribute Post-it notes or small slips of paper that can be taped onto the map.

■ Markers and highlighters can be used to show trends, influences, and connections.

■ The map could be redrawn as a class project at the end of the unit, providing an excellent review for everyone.

■ You might also provide a skeleton map that shows a basic shape as a sample of a mind map configuration.

■ You can give students maps that begin to demonstrate mapping a topic that they are studying and then ask them to add branches as they fill in the details.

■ You, the teacher, can provide maps that preview what will be learned or to review a subject, event, or discussion.

■ You might model mapping on the board as students share their ideas. In this setting the mapping serves as a record of the discussion or brainstorming session. Students gain receptive skills first and later produce their own maps (expressive skills).

The more you use mapping for your personal and professional needs, the better prepared you will be to teach it and to help your students find applications that meet their needs. If you haven't already jumped ahead and begun your own map, now is the time. The map on the opposite page will remind you of the key points to keep in mind while mapping.

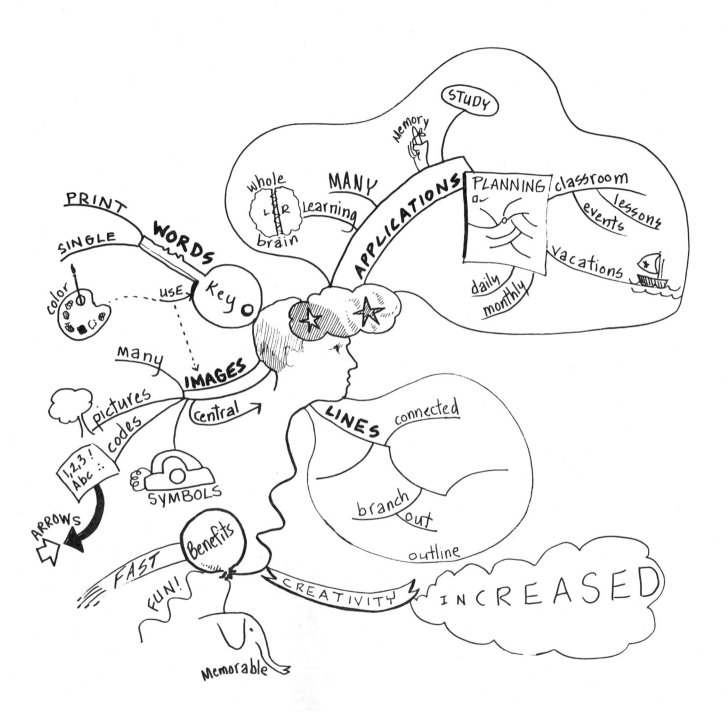

Chapter 2

Symbols and Drawing

Symbols and You

You don't have to be a great artist in order to draw symbols for mind maps. If you are uncomfortable about drawing and feel awkward even trying it, you are in good company. Most people believe that they can't draw and gave up on themselves as potential artists by the age of nine or ten. In fact, drawing is a skill that comes naturally to very few people. However, it is, like reading and math, a subject that can be *learned*. All you need is a willingness to develop your ability to be a "visual thinker." The more you create mind maps, the better able you will be to represent your thoughts with pictures.

■ For the purpose of mind mapping, you can develop very simple drawing techniques that will enable you to copy and create a variety of symbols. Look at the space around you. Do you see any symbols, logos, book covers, or designs that might be useful for mind mapping? As you read magazines, begin to notice the myriad of symbols, designs, and simple pictures that abound. Driving down the street, you will see a growing number of traffic signs that are purely visual and can be understood without the use of written words. There are symbols for everything from rest room signs to emergency instructions in airplanes.

■ You can begin now practicing symbol gathering. When you read the word "LOVE," what visual image do you have? Can you simplify it? Many people see a heart; others might see a face, two people, or a flower.

■ Think about the word "MONEY." Lots of money. Did you come up with a dollar sign, a bag, a stack of bills, or coins? Grab a paper and pencil and sketch a symbol for money. What about lots of money coming your way unexpectedly? Perhaps you envision it falling from the sky or heaping up all around you. Use your imagination and before drawing an image, mentally review as many symbols as you can envision for "lots of money."

An important part of becoming facile with symbol making is developing the ability to run through a number of images mentally, selecting the one that meets two important criteria: it conveys your meaning, and it is within your ability to draw on paper. I find that over the years I have settled on a set of symbols that I can draw rapidly and remember easily. You can see them on the opposite page.

Beyond that set, I find new symbols appearing

everyday in the environment and on the maps I create. An important plus of mind mapping is that it encourages you to develop another language — your own, personal, visual language.

Step-by-Step Symbol Making

For many of us drawing people is one of the biggest challenges in drawing. Here is one simple method that I find useful. Heads, as you can see, can be represented by a circle when facing forward. An oval will work well, too.

To show that a person is a child, simply place the eyes below the half way point, make the nose small and add a curl on top for babies.

When drawing the head from the side, a circle is fine, but an oval doesn't work as well. Feel the back of your head and you will find that it bulges out quite a bit and is much narrower where it joins the spine. This shape can be conveyed by adding a circle overlapping the oval shape.

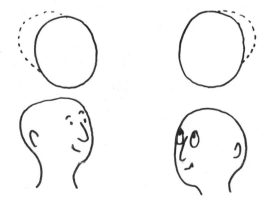

Handy Signs:

You draw the shapes here
⇩

Variations:

Draw the "Essence" of Elephant. Sometimes you don't need to draw the entire object to convey the idea.

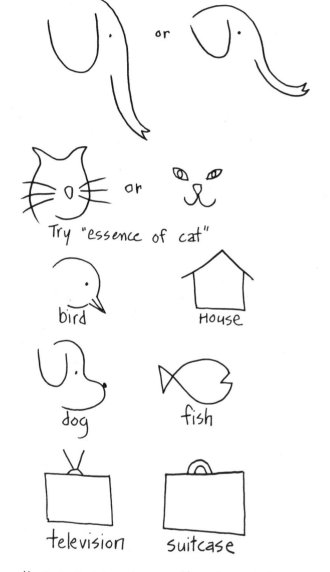

or

Try "essence of cat"

bird

House

dog

fish

One way to loosen up your image-making abilities is to create a visual record of the most important moments in your life. See if you can come up with a symbolic way to represent each major event in your life.

As you can see on this page, you can represent an object or concept with very few lines. Rather than drawing an entire elephant to represent MEMORY, I draw the "essence of elephant."

The following pages are designed for you, so you can practice drawing simple symbols, one element at a time. The exercises combine simple shapes and step-by-step combinations of shapes. You may notice that the "copy the shape" method looks rather childish, but remember the last time you drew for the fun of it, without judging your work. For most of us that time was when we were age ten or eleven. Close your eyes, remember yourself at that age, then open your eyes and copy the symbols in the book with the attitude and enthusiasm of that younger you.

person   child   crowd   television   suitcase

notice that more people, in the back of the crowd, are a simple "⌒"

40

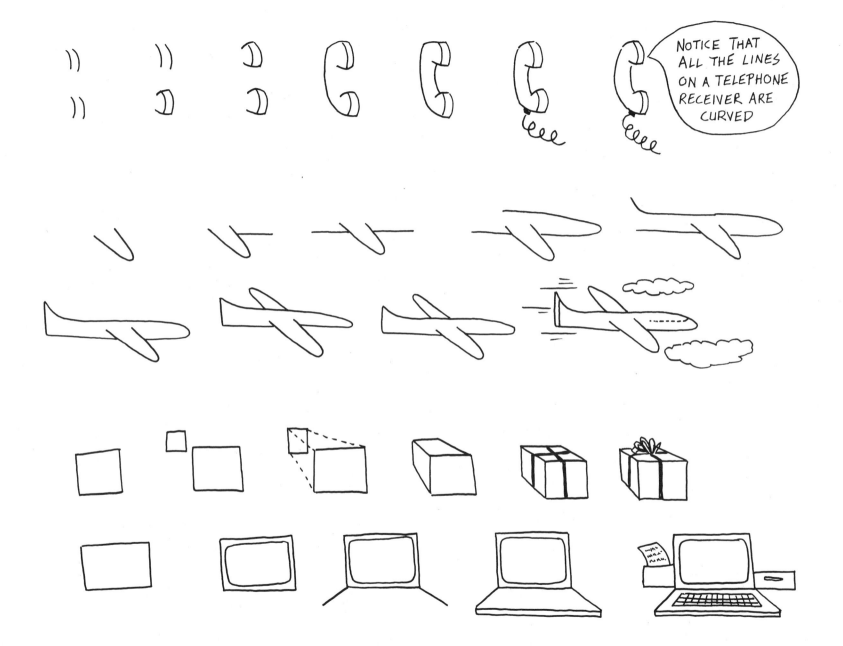

41

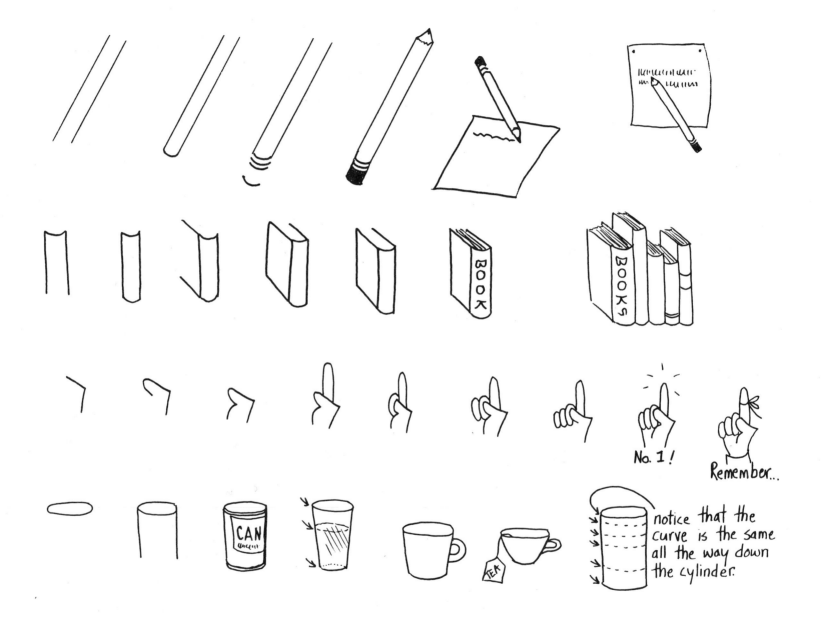

No. 1!

Remember...

CAN

TEA

notice that the curve is the same all the way down the cylinder.

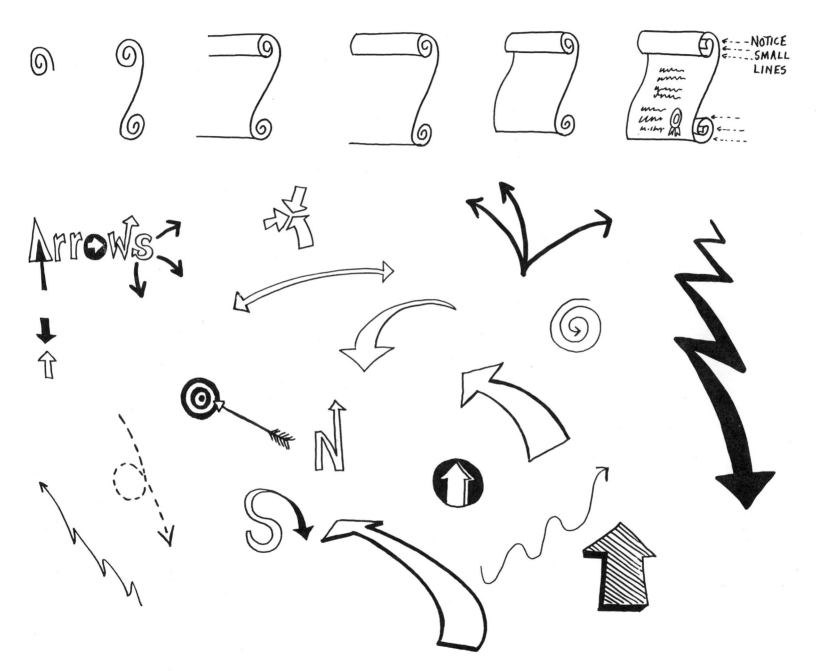

NOTICE
SMALL
LINES

Arrows

Often a word can be drawn in a manner that conveys its meaning.

To add dimension to a word, use another color or a thicker line on the top and left

practice drawing oval shapes, moving your entire arm while drawing.

use the ovals to create cylindrical forms.

the curve of the label is the same as the curve of the can.

Now try variations:

Add shading, using a pencil to vary the shades of gray.

Hey, I can draw!

Yes, you CAN!

CAN

the can that is higher and darker appears to be behind the other can.

flag hide friend

Worldsign

David Orcutt of British Columbia has developed an entire language of symbols that are most useful for mind mapping. His language, called Worldsign, goes far beyond individual symbols and has the potential of becoming a global language. For every written symbol in Worldsign there is a matching gesture. This means that one can either write or sign in Worldsign. The Worldsign symbols can also be animated for film, video, and computers. When mind mapping, you may wish to use some of the symbols from Worldsign.

Worldsign makes use of three types of symbols: kinegraphs, ideographs, and pictographs. The kinegraphs are based on manual signs from a number of sign languages from around the world. Ideographs are symbols that we commonly use, such as stars and hearts. Pictographs are pictures that have been pared down to their essential elements. (Orcutt 1987)

On this page are pictographs from Worldsign that are useful for mind mapping. Page 47 is designed so that you can photocopy it and challenge your class to name each symbol.

nose

door floor roof

eye

rain year cow cup

see night glasses energy

telephone animal bird cook

fall dance scales heavy

comb person people meet past future bend bow

Guess what each of these Worldsign symbols mean.

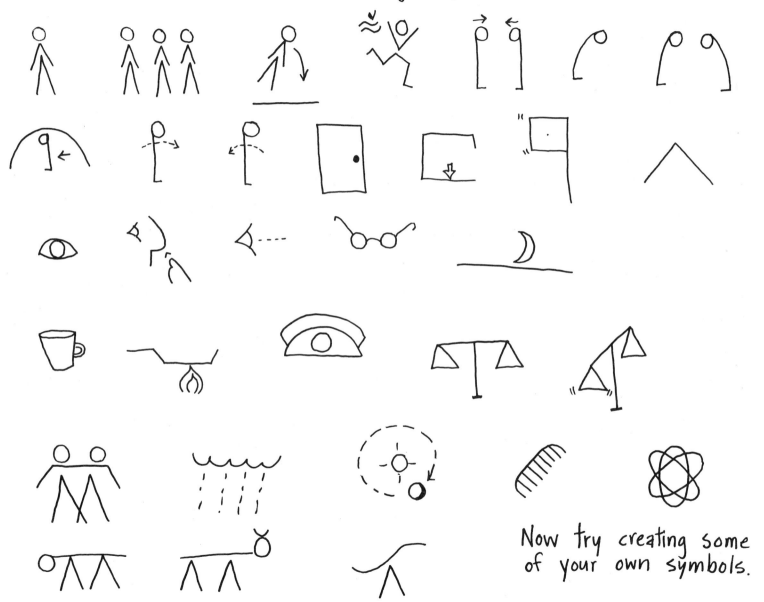

Now try creating some of your own symbols.

47

Chapter 3

Introducing Mind Mapping to Students

There are a number of ways to introduce mind mapping to your students. I have included here several exciting approaches. Choose the one that suits you and your students best. Though approximate age levels are suggested, most activities can be adjusted to suit other levels.

As you have seen, mind mapping uses key words and does not require the use of phrases, a knowledge of grammar, or English literacy. Thus, mapping can be used before children become literate in English. Mapping capitalizes on a child's delight in color, symbols, and imagery.

The use of symbols, such as stars, hearts, and faces, gives children the opportunity to experience the basis of language before moving to the more complex task of writing English. This symbolic thinking with visual images representing ideas precedes the use of spoken language and does not have to be lost when we learn to read and write.

If we see the purpose of written language as a tool for recording and communicating our ideas, why not motivate and excite children with an intriguing yet simple method to convey *their* ideas? There is no need to limit their expression of ideas to words and phrases.

Day One

This exercise will introduce mind mapping on a basic level and enable students to play with the nonlinear arrangement of ideas on paper before learning the specifics of mind mapping.

A good warm-up to mind mapping, this activity is also an excellent getting-to-know-you exercise.

Materials needed

for each student:
* 10-12 circles , cut from assorted colors of construction paper, in sizes varying from one to three inches
  1 sheet unlined paper, 11" x 17"
  crayons or colored markers
  1 glue stick

* If you prefer, simply draw circles on a master sheet (8 1/2" x 11"), photocopy on colored sheets, and ask students to cut out their own.

To introduce younger students to mind mapping, demonstrate this activity on a flip chart or chalkboard.

■ Ask each child to select a circle that represents himself or herself and one circle for each person, place, or

MANY

classroom
home
Activities

INTRODUCTION

KIDS

enjoy

IDEAS   MINE!

MY OWN!

SYMBOLS   visual

DOG CAT RUN

The dog and the cat run

DOG CAT RUN

Prewriting   Prereading

ie:

FUN

"DAY ONE"

+++ KNOW   others

UNDERSTAND   self

activity

BASIC

"premapping"

MATERIALS

color

SizE   vary

GLUE STICK

11" x 17"

OR

CRAYONS

Markers

49

thing that is important in his or her life. The size of the circles can be used to show relative importance to the student.

■ For example, a child might select circles for Self, Mom, Dad, sister, brother, Cub Scouts, school, baseball, friends, and pet.

■ The circles should then be placed on a large sheet of paper and moved around until their relative positions reflect the child's relationship to each of these things.

■ You might want to ask children to look at the positions and decide if they are the right distance from each other. Is anything too close or too far away? Should any of these shapes be closer to each other, like Mom and your sister, or baseball and friends?

■ When children are satisfied with the relative placement of their shapes, they should be glued in place.

■ Crayons and markers can be used to draw lines, arrows, and other connecting marks between the circles. If children wish, they can draw images or symbols on the circles. As you can imagine, this exercise will give you insight into your students and help them see the "larger" picture of their lives.

■ A variation on this is to make a similar pattern-map of how the child would *like* his or her world to be. Ask children: What changes in the relative distance and connections would be ideal? What would you like to add?

Beginning Maps

Materials needed:
For each student:
   unlined paper (preferably 11 x 17")
   colored pencils or medium felt-tip markers

For the teacher:
   unlined paper 26" x 33" (flip chart size)
   broad-tip colored markers for highlighting
   colored chalk for use at chalkboard

The Classroom Environment
When teaching mapping, make sure that everyone has sufficient table or desk space for a large sheet of paper and several markers. Children might find it handy to keep markers in a plastic cup on the table.

When your goal is to generate the maximum number of creative ideas, take time to create an environment that is relaxing, comfortable, and safe. To accomplish this, you might play some classical music or instrumentals such as the Windham Hill series. Pachelbel's *Canon*, Handel's *Water Music*, and Beethoven's *Emperor Concerto* are excellent for this exercise. This music connects to the intuitive, artistic parts of the brain and promotes creative thinking.

Naturally, the room should be a comfortable temperature and the light adequate.

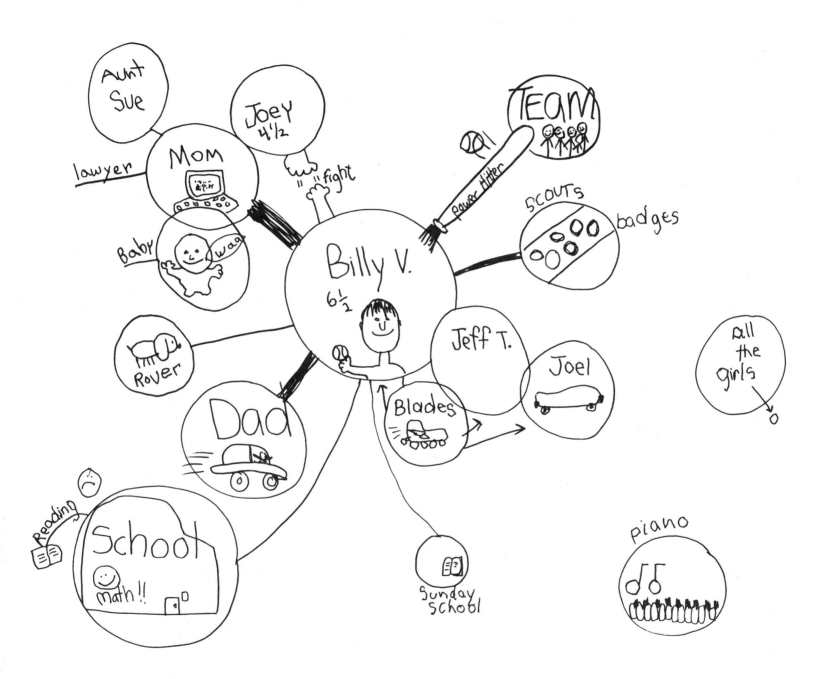

51

Some children work best if they are not at a table, but rather sitting or lying on the floor. Mapping can be one of the activities in which everyone is free to work in whatever position works best for the individual. Those children who need to take frequent breaks or like to move around could be allowed to get up, stretch, and look at the work of other students. There may be a student who works best standing at an easel. When that can be arranged, let students experiment with standing at an easel or working with colored chalk on the board.

When students are creating their first maps, the subject should be an easy one. Some topics that I find work well for first maps are:

▶ things I can do

▶ who I am (my interests, goals, skills, friends, family purpose, values,)

▶ what I did yesterday (last week, this month)

▶ what I want in the future

▶ all that I would like to learn (do, be, have)

Notice that all these topics are based upon the children's own thoughts and ideas. Later, when the process is more comfortable for them, students can map topics that they are studying in school and take notes in mind map form during classroom presentations.

The First Steps

It is helpful to show your students a simple mind map before they begin. Create your map as you talk, drawing on the board or on a flip chart.

■ Ask children to begin mapping by drawing a central symbol that represents their topic. Remind them to draw their symbol in the middle of the page. If students can't think of a picture to begin their maps, suggest that they just draw a simple shape and fill in the symbol drawing later.

■ Explain that they may use key words as well as symbols as they branch out from the central image.

■ Invite them to use colors freely. (As they gain experience, colors can be used for coding and highlighting.)

■ Encourage children to write all the ideas that come to them, even the ones that seem far-fetched or silly. Drawings need not be fancy or polished; children can cross out words if a mistake is made. Students will be surprised to learn that "messy" is acceptable, a new rule for most!

At first, children may not branch from key words; their maps tend to look like simple hubs with spokes. I remind them that they can branch out, like tree branches grow from main limbs, and show them a sample "skeleton mind map" to illustrate this point. The skeleton map shows how lines can be curved to avoid the

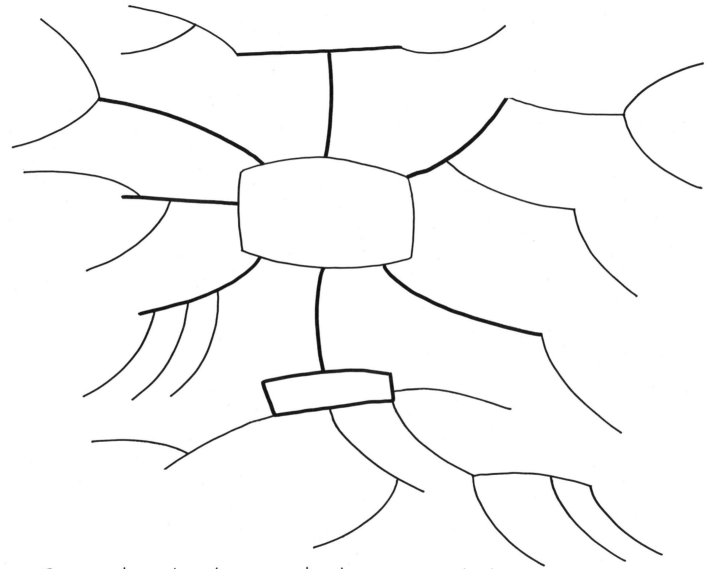

MIND MAPS can branch out in any direction. Curving the lines makes it easier to write every word right side up. Boxes around words are also useful.

tendency to write sideways and upside-down while constructing a map. With curved lines and a "T" shape moving up directly from the central image, all words can be written right side up. This makes the map easier to construct and much easier to read later.

∎ You may wish to give each learner a copy of a skeleton mind map and a copy of the mind map on the subject of mind mapping.

Demonstrating

When I visit an elementary school to teach mapping, I often begin by making several sample maps.

∎ After explaining to the children that I am going to show them a new and exciting way to write ideas, I ask them to think of a subject that interests them. The topics they choose may range from soccer to science, Pee Wee Herman to computers. The only qualification is that they must know enough about the subject to tell me about it. For instance, one class might select science as a favorite subject. (I hope they will say the same when they reach 10th grade!)

∎ To map science, first discuss all the images that come to mind about SCIENCE. At this point I sometimes jump-start their imaginations by asking them to close their eyes and see what pictures pop into their minds when the word SCIENCE is spoken. I say the word with several different tones of voice: booming, whispered, impor-

tantly, laughingly, slowly, or in a computer-like voice. I stop each time after saying the word.

∎ Students who have an image in mind can raise their hands and tell the group what appeared to them. As they share their visions, I draw them on the board. To draw the images, one does not need to be an artist. Just a simple representation will do. Often a child will gladly come to the board and draw an image. Colored chalk adds to the fun. While one child draws an image, others close their eyes and continue the creative visualization process.

∎ A variation on this: ask the children to listen with eyes closed. Each time they see an image in their mind's eye, they open their eyes and draw that image on a sheet of paper.

This process alone, which precedes teaching mapping, is excellent for developing one of the skills that is important to learning: the ability to visualize. A key aspect of creativity, visualizing can be employed throughout life.

∎ Now that you have tapped the children's creative genius (not bad for a half hour's work), you can then select a central image from among those that the students have suggested. In the sample map included on page 57, the image is a combination of a test tube and a sort of robot.

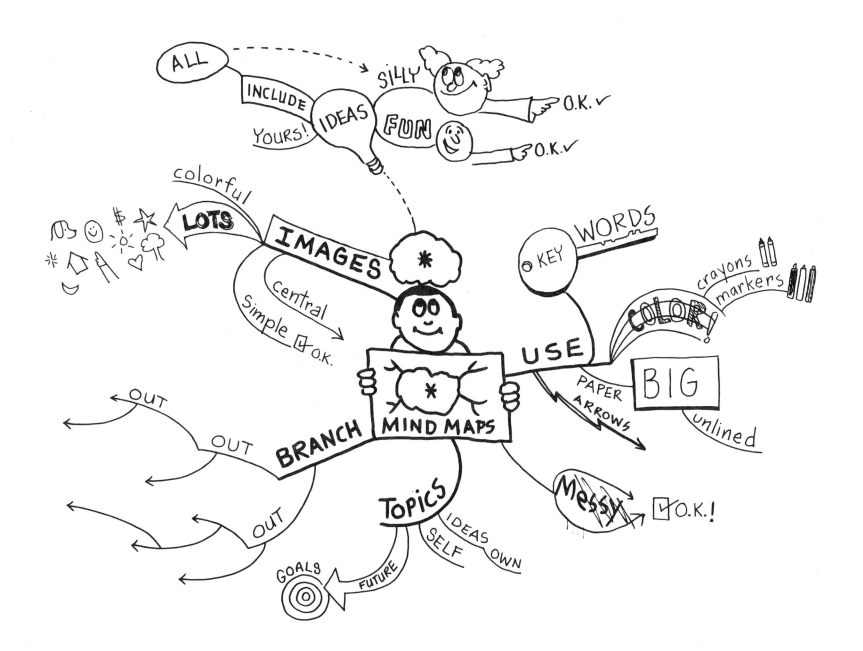

ALL

INCLUDE

IDEAS

YOURS!

SILLY

FUN

O.K. ✓

O.K. ✓

colorful

LOTS

IMAGES

central

Simple ☑ O.K.

KEY WORDS

USE

COLOR!

crayons

markers

BIG

unlined

OUT

OUT

BRANCH

MIND MAPS

PAPER

ARROWS

Messy

☑ O.K.!

OUT

TOPICS

IDEAS OWN

SELF

GOALS

FUTURE

■ With the central image in place, open the discussion to free associations. For this phase of generating ideas I ask children to tell me what ideas come to mind when they look at the image on the board. I explain that when we do this, any idea that occurs to them is fine. There are no right or wrong answers. We will list all ideas without stopping to comment or criticize.

As we focused on SCIENCE, one child suggested that scientists experiment with making weird mixtures. Instead of writing the entire phrase, I selected a key word and wrote EXPERIMENT. The word MIXTURES branched from EXPERIMENT. Next we discussed what other experiments scientists make.

"Sometimes they experiment with drinking mixtures and turning into monsters like Dr. Seek and Mr. Hide," one student informed me. Since that is more science fiction, I suggested that FICTION become another branch of the map.

"They experiment with animals, like teaching a monkey to type," one child reported. Good! ANIMALS became a branch off the word experiment. (I explained that typing was not within the skills of monkeys, to the best of my knowledge, but teaching apes to use sign language is.) A few of the students had heard about that. I asked them for ideas about how to draw an ape. The arms are long, the head is large, and the body is hairy. I proceeded to draw an ape.

■ In cases like this, teachers can feel free to ask students for assistance, and more importantly, the teacher's willingness to draw pictures on the board that are not perfect is a real plus. Students can see that you are learning, too, and are willing to take risks or ask for assistance from the group.

As the map on the next page demonstrates, my group of science buffs came up with a great range of topics related to science. When they mentioned plants, I supplied the word BOTANY and reinforced it with lots of flowers and trees. For studying living things, I explained BIOLOGY. At that point I explained that any key word could become the center of a new map. For example, biology could be a central image, with all the associations to that topic filling the board.

■ This demonstration process can be repeated as often as you like. A second map might be created as a group of students recall the elements of a story that was read to them. As you explain a topic, ask your class to suggest the next branch or advise you where the next piece of information could be added to the map.

■ Older students can review all the facts of a subject they recently studied while you map on the chalkboard and act as their mind map scribe. To preview or review a subject you can make maps on large sheets or rolls of white butcher paper to display in the room. You can refer to a map not only for review, but also to show the class

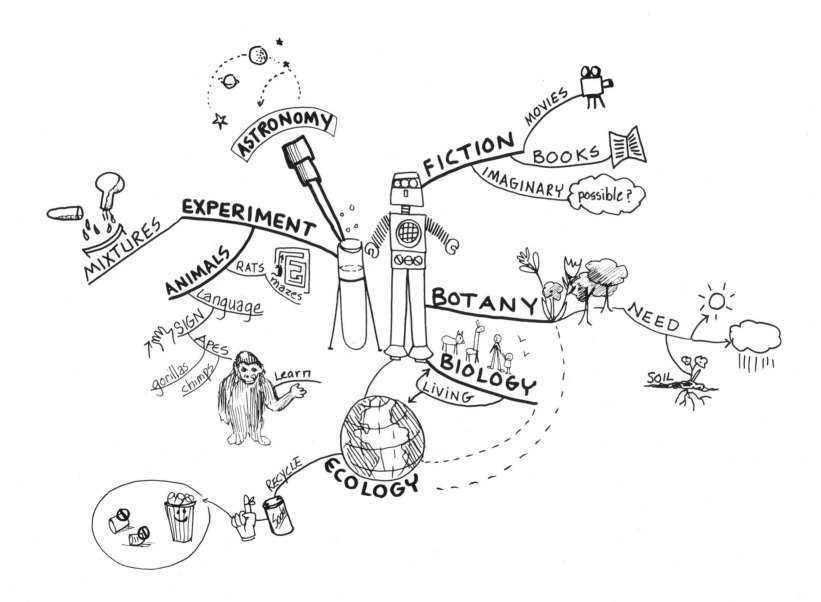

ASTRONOMY

FICTION
MOVIES
BOOKS
IMAGINARY possible?

EXPERIMENT

MIXTURES

ANIMALS
RATS
mazes
Language
SIGN
Apes
gorillas chimps
Learn

BOTANY

NEED
SOIL

BIOLOGY
Living

ECOLOGY
RECYCLE
Soda

where to add a new fact or facet of the subject as it is introduced. After a map is posted in the room, it can be seen, not as finished, but as representing an ongoing process (like learning itself). Students can add Post-it notes or their own symbols and words as their understanding or recall deepens.

Experiencing

Materials needed:
For each student:
    unlined paper (11" x 17")
    crayons or colored pens
    glitter glue stick (nice to have)

For the teacher:
    "a magic wand"

I have also found that children can move into mapping from an entirely different direction: that of pure experience. In this approach I do not explain terms such a mind mapping or suggest that we are learning a new system.

■ Instead, I come into the room with my handy magic wand and explain that I am the Fairy Godmother and plan to grant unlimited wishes to everyone in the room.

■ Each student is then instructed to take one large sheet of paper and in the center draw an image that represents magic. This could be anything: a star, a wand, a magician's top hat.

■ From this image I ask the students to draw pictures representing the things they wish for. I suggest that they use lines to connect each wish to the magic source in the center.

■ I remind them to use color, and I sometimes provide glitter glue sticks for that added dash of magic. This exercise is an entertaining one and introduces mind mapping in an important context: as connected to the creative imagination and individuality of the child.

Discovering

Introduce your older students to mind mapping by challenging them with the notion that our usual methods of note-taking and writing papers don't work very well. Begin with a list of all the problems involved in note-*taking* (writing your own ideas on paper) or the problems of note-*making* (recording the ideas of others from lectures or books). The class will generate ideas such as:

▶ It's difficult to get started.

▶ The process is too slow.

▶ In class, it's hard to listen and record ideas at the same time.

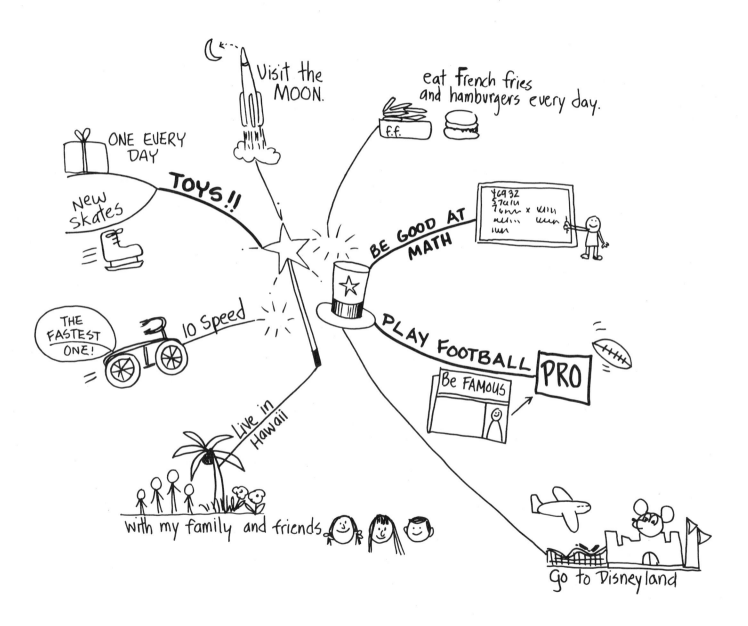

- My notes do not assist me in remembering material.
- Note-taking is boring.
- There is no way to fit new ideas in where they belong in the notes.
- It's hard to get an overview.
- It is difficult to think of ideas in the right order.

■ After listing all the limitations of traditional note-taking and note-making, suggest that these drawbacks can be seen as challenges in disguise. For example, the problem, "it's hard to get started" could become the challenge: create a system that is fun and makes it easy to get started. This new system would have to be fast, easy, and memorable.

■ The entire group might then brainstorm a new system, or you might divide the class into cooperative learning groups of three or four students. Groups would invent their own systems and create a sample of the system to show the rest of the class. As in all cooperative learning groups, each person in the group should be able to explain the new system and tell why and how it was created.

I have found that when we combine the best of each group's new systems, we come up with something that is surprisingly similar to mind mapping.

■ After this exercise is completed, you can explain that the mind mapping system was created by Tony Buzan, the noted author and researcher. In most cases you will be able to compliment the class for inventing a system to rival one developed by a man who is known throughout the world for his creative genius.

Explaining the Brain to Students

Since some students are using their brains in an unaccustomed fashion when mind mapping, you may wish to explain to them how the brain works. I encourage you to read Barbara Clark's *Optimizing Learning* for some excellent information on teaching children about their brains.

For the purpose of introducing mind mapping, I suggest that you explain the basics of whole-brain learning so that students can understand why the creative and intuitive aspects of their brains are engaged in mind mapping. The left and right hemisphere theory is so easy to misunderstand or oversimplify that I usually avoid it by saying something like the following:

"Your brain has many ways to take in information from within you and from the outside world. For one part of your brain imagine standing on the top of a beautiful mountain. Feel the air against your skin…hear music played somewhere far away…smell the flowers…see the whole view of trees, flowers, a village, a valley and more mountains in the distance. The colors you

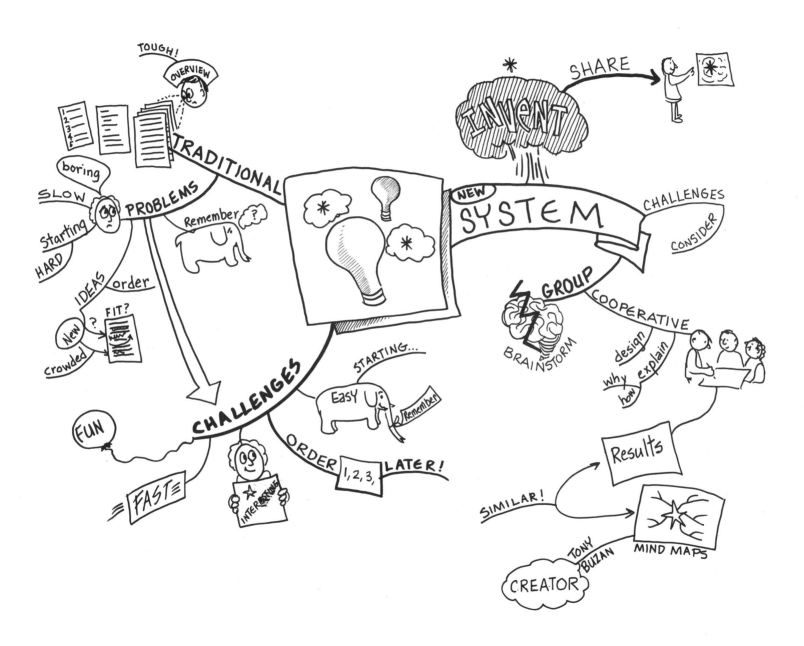

TOUGH!

OVERVIEW

TRADITIONAL

boring

SLOW

PROBLEMS

Starting

HARD

Remember

IDEAS   order

FIT?

New   ?

Crowded

FUN

FAST

CHALLENGES

INTERESTING

STARTING...

Easy   Remember

ORDER 1, 2, 3, LATER!

INVENT

SHARE

NEW   SYSTEM

CHALLENGES

CONSIDER

GROUP

COOPERATIVE

BRAINSTORM

design

why   explain

how

Results

SIMILAR!

MIND MAPS

CREATOR   TONY BUZAN

see are wonderful…beautiful blues, many different shades of green and purple. Imagine what it might be like to be in the village below, as you look at the sky above and picture yourself flying through the clouds in a magical flying machine.

That part of your brain likes to take in the whole picture, dream of things you can't see but can imagine, and feel feelings, even when you don't have words to describe them.

Another part of your brain has a different way of taking in information:

Imagine now that you are in a big building. There are rows of doors on both sides of the hallway. As you walk down the hall, you can go into any door. Count your steps as you walk along, 1, 2, 3, 4. Then go into a room and find it full of big file cabinets…Open a drawer and there, neatly printed, is a page of typewritten information. You read what it says…Open another drawer that has folders that are numbered, 1 to 1,000! Notice, too, that there is a large clock in this room and you can hear it ticking. This part of your brain learns in an orderly 1, 2, 3 way: the part that helps you keep track of time and pay attention to your teacher!

Luckily, we all have brains that can do many things; imagine, add numbers, remember songs, write poems, play soccer, and learn the rules, too.

The part of our brain that can look at the "big picture" works with the part that takes in information in an orderly neat fashion."

I also tell the students:

"When you want to think of ideas for writing a paper, you need your whole brain to help you think of good ideas and put them in order. Mind mapping helps you do that. First, mapping appeals to the creative part of you by using color, large sheets of paper, pictures, and no special order. Later, you can use the more logical, 1,2,3 part of your brain to decide which ideas are best and put them in order. That way your whole brain is encouraged to help you first think of many good ideas and see the connections among them and then decide which ideas are best and put them in order.

Mind mapping, because it uses color and pictures, makes remembering easier, too. If I ask you to think of the last chapter you studied in your social studies book, or the last library book you read, most of you think of a picture — maybe the cover of the book or an illustration. Not many people think of a sentence or paragraph of the book. So, when we use pictures, we are giving our memories a better chance to recall the ideas later."

Barbara Clark, building on an idea from Dr. Paul McLean, suggests that you use your hands to explain the functions of the brain to older students.

■ To create a model of the human brain, put your hands together, thumbs visible and touching each other.

■ Wiggle the little fingers, and you have identified the area through which vision enters the brain.

■ Think of each hand as representing one hemisphere, with the fingernails representing the corpus callosum, which sends impulses back and forth between the two hemispheres.

■ Your middle finger is the motor area. The language area is just below the middle knuckle on the left hand.

■ Now open the hands and look at your wrist and arm. These represent the brainstem which is the simplest and most primitive system of the brain. This part of the brain evolved more than five hundred million years ago. It is called the reptilian brain because it resembles the entire brain of a reptile. We do not consciously think about every breath we take, or every beat of the heart. The brainstem takes care of these automatic functions. Here we also find neural pathways for many higher brain centers. The reticulate formation is here, too. It is responsible for keeping us awake and alert.

■ Partially unclench your fist and you look at the palm of either hand to see the limbic system. It attaches to the rear of the brainstem. This area regulates hormones and sexual functions and affects a wide range of emotions. This system gives us our sense of individual identity and provides the bridge between our inner and outer worlds. Feelings of pleasure and joy as well as novelty stimulate this area.

■ We receive, store, and recall information in the cerebrum. This largest area of the brain is represented by the exposed surface of your fingers and thumb held tightly together. This area comprises five-sixths of the brain and envelops the lower brainstem and limbic system. It is divided into two halves or hemispheres. Speech, language, decision making, and action taking are located here.

■ Covering each hemisphere is a one-eighth-inch thick layer of nerve cells called the cortex. We are able to create, organize ideas, remember, and communicate with the help of the cortex.

■ Each hemisphere is divided into four areas or lobes. The frontal, represented by the thumbs, enables us to plan, decide upon an action, have insights, and be intuitive. The parietal lobe relates to body position and touch. The temporal lobe is related to memory, hearing, and perception. The occipital lobe is related to vision and reading.

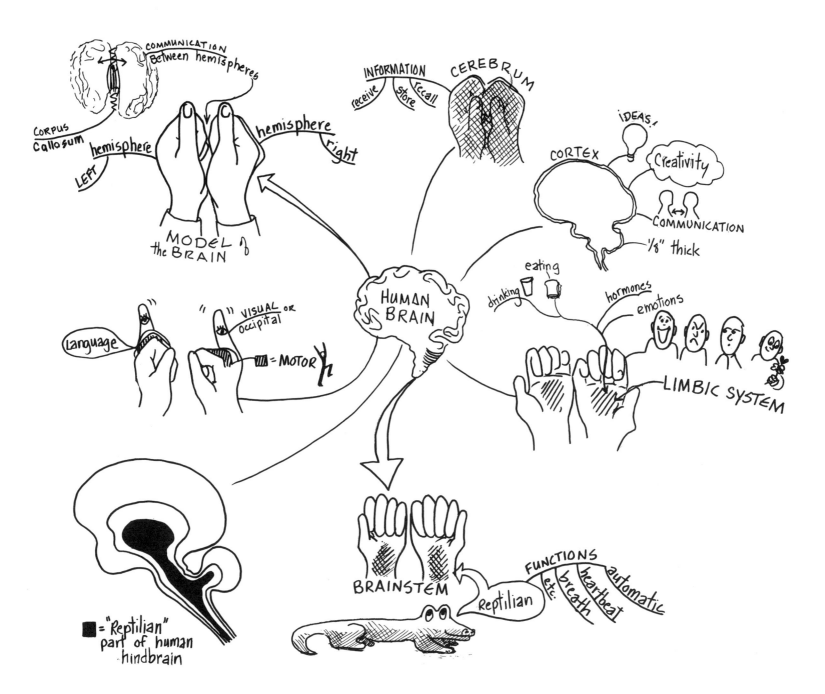

COMMUNICATION
Between hemispheres

CORPUS
Callosum

hemisphere
LEFT

hemisphere
right

MODEL of
the BRAIN

INFORMATION
receive   store   recall

CEREBRUM

CORTEX

IDEAS!

Creativity

COMMUNICATION

1/8" thick

Language

" " VISUAL OR
occipital

= MOTOR

HUMAN
BRAIN

eating

drinking

hormones

emotions

LIMBIC SYSTEM

= "Reptilian"
part of human
hindbrain

BRAINSTEM

Reptilian

FUNCTIONS
etc.   breath   heartbeat   automatic

Braingloves

■ With younger students I use gloves that are decorated to make learning about the brain more fun and memorable. "Brain Gloves" are made from inexpensive white cotton gloves that are decorated with fabric markers, (available in art supply or fabric stores.) The gloves can include eyes from the craft shop, a name tag, and drawings and symbols to represent each aspect described above.

■ Older children can invent their own gloves and use them to explain the workings of the brain to younger children.

■ When new information about the workings of our brains appears in the press, share it with your students. You can make a mind map about brain facts or brain theories and add to it as new information becomes available.

■ It's fun to challenge your class to imagine what brain facts scientists might uncover in the future. The title of such a map might be: "The Amazing Brain — Discoveries in the year 2020."

Whatever the focus of your studies of the brain, the primary goal is to insure that each of us realizes the vast, unlimited potential we possess. Using the hands as a model of the brain, remind students that we use less than 1 percent of the brain's potential — the equivalent of slightly wiggling one finger.

Every mind map is a view into the highly unique territory created by our own amazing brains — into the uncharted inner space that we all possess.

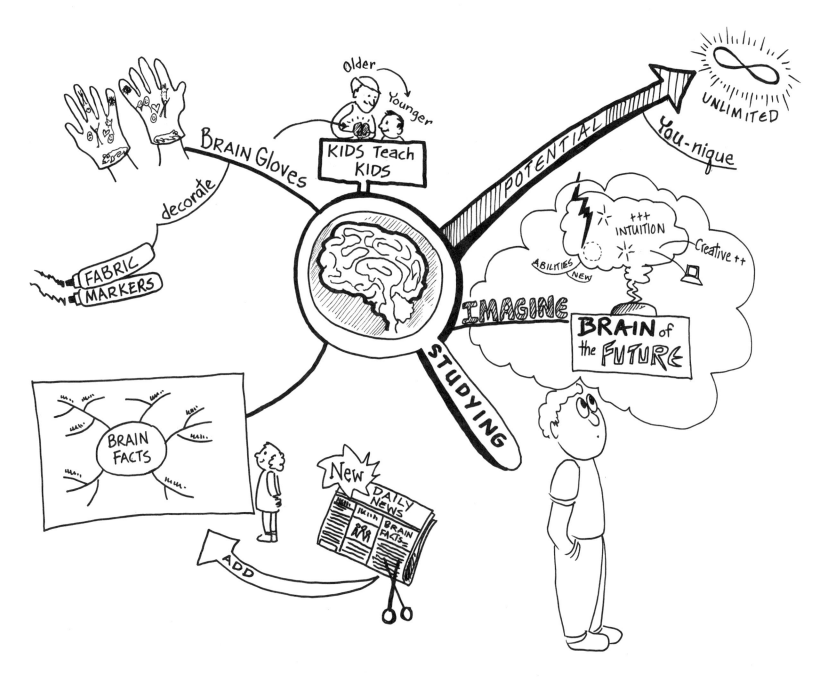

Brain Gloves

decorate

FABRIC MARKERS

Older → Younger

KIDS Teach KIDS

POTENTIAL

You-nique

UNLIMITED

IMAGINE

INTUITION +++

ABILITIES NEW

Creative ++

BRAIN of the FUTURE

STUDYING

BRAIN FACTS

New

DAILY NEWS

BRAIN FACTS

ADD

Chapter 4

Symbols and Students

You can introduce symbol drawing to the group before they make their own maps or afterward. Often children create their own symbols and share them with each other. If a group of symbols is given at the beginning, children may be less creative in developing personal ones.

I suggest to my students that they take time to see their world differently — in terms of visual symbols.

■ If time permits, take a walk with your class through the building or outside to see what symbols you can find.

■ Younger children enjoy making rubbings from gratings, walls, license plates, and other surfaces with a raised design or logo. To accomplish this, each child needs a large sheet of newsprint and a crayon with the paper peeled off. The child can then put the paper on top of the surface and rub across it with the side of the crayon until the image appears clearly.

■ Back in the classroom, children can compare the results of their "symbol search" and test each other to see if they can remember where the image came from.

Young Children

Materials needed:
a supply of index cards

You can lead young students through an activity that encourages them to create their own symbols for persons, places, and topics that are of special importance to them.

■ Give children a series of index cards and instruct them to draw a symbol on each card that represents themselves, their family, their school, as well as concepts such as feeling happy or worried, or studying, thinking, or learning.

■ You may wish to help them generate the list of topics with the whole class brainstorming. Then ask students to work on their own individual symbol cards. The symbols that each child creates for a topic such as "school" or "our class" could be compared or displayed. The class could select certain symbols that would be used for group mind mapping.

■ Another way to encourage young children to begin symbol making is to brainstorm possible symbols, asking the students to come to the chalkboard and draw

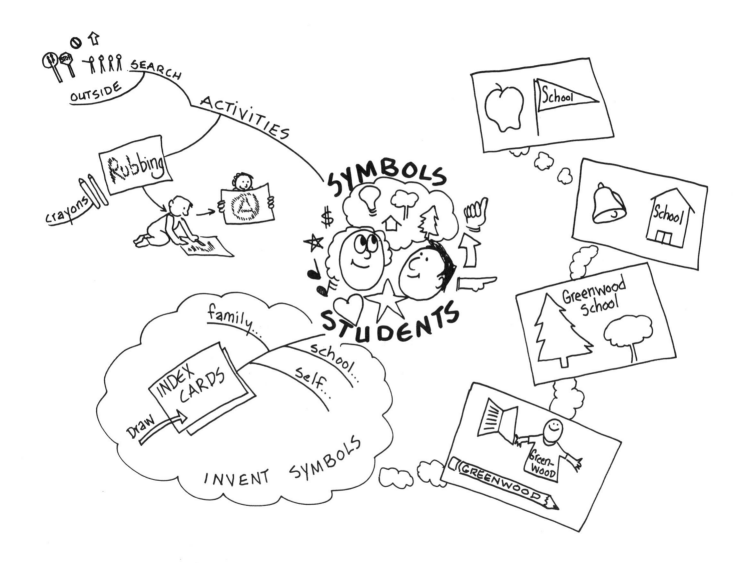

their ideas for the rest of the class to see. These symbols can then be copied and reproduced on a sheet that each student can cut and paste when making a map. I recommend that students be encouraged to add their own new symbols as well as special lines, arrows, and codes, even when pasting together a first map.

Older Students

Materials needed:
a supply of index cards
an egg timer

A great introduction to symbol making (and team playing) is *Pictionary*, a game that requires players to draw an image that their teammates must guess. You might want to buy a game for your class to use during an inside recess or create a game to use with your students.

▮ To make the game, cut index cards in half and write a word or phrase on each card. Your students can make up their own cards and contribute to creating the game. Any word that you feel the students could possibly represent with a drawing could be included.

▮ Divide the group into two or three teams and decide who goes first. Use the egg timer for limiting each turn.

▮ The first player selects a card and shows it to one member of the other team.

▮ The players who have seen the word then draw as rapidly as they can while their teammates try to guess the right word. Each member of a team gets a turn to draw the words or phrases.

▮ A great review tactic is to create a Historical Events Pictionary, or one related to other curriculum areas.

▮ You can also use a chalkboard to set up a game like the television show, "Win, Lose or Draw."

▮ Another way to loosen up image-making abilities is to create a visual record of the most important moments in one's life.

▮ In a classroom setting students can be asked to create picture-portraits of their lives and then share the results with a couple of other people. The advantage of this exercise is that students can pick up ideas from each other on symbolic drawings and get to know each other better in the process.

Hieroglyphics

Your students might enjoy studying ancient Egyptian hieroglyphics to see how a symbol system can work. One hieroglyph can evoke a wealth of meaning.

Students can make up their own hieroglyphs beginning with a symbol of any sort in the center of a page.

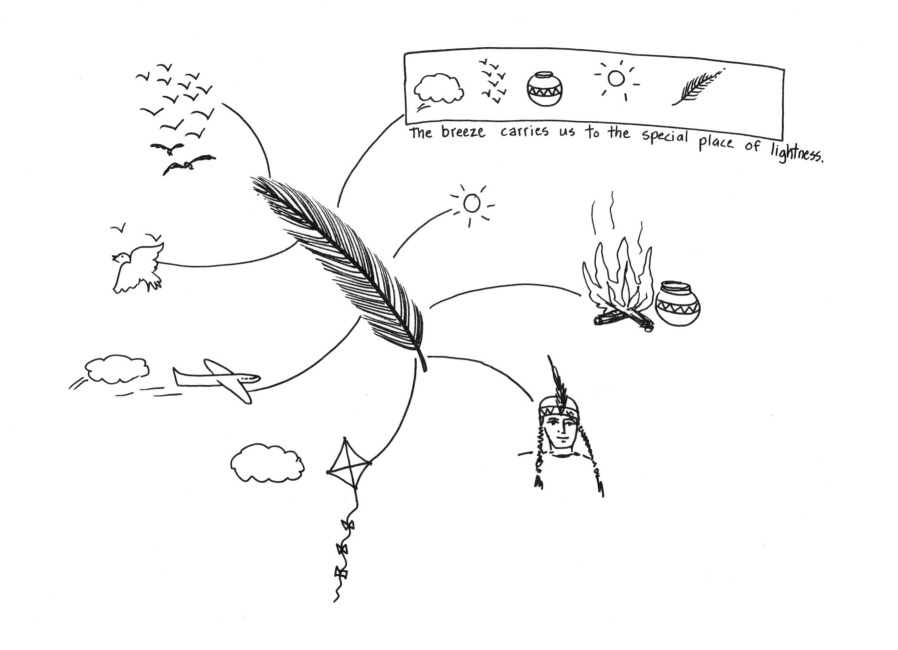

The breeze carries us to the special place of lightness.

From that simple drawing they should draw any other idea or image that occurs to them. For example, I might draw a feather in the center of my paper. In association with the feather, I might think of a bird and draw a bird on a line connected to the feather. Next, I might think of flight and draw an airplane. Other associations might lead me to air, flock, Indian, or ceremony. Each of these is represented on my paper by an image or glyph as shown in the mind map on page 71.

When the associations are complete, I can make a sentence from a string of hieroglyphs, using only the images on my paper. Next, I can look again at the hieroglyph sentence and write it in English words.

To challenge children's creative imagination, this exercise can be carried a step further. The next step is to see oneself from the point of view of the central image. Tell your students to ask themselves: How would I appear if viewed by a bird, a feather, or a house? Demonstrate this on the chalkboard.

At the board, draw yourself from this odd vantage point and then repeat the process, drawing each association in image only (no words) and then constructing a sentence from those images. I can draw myself as seen by a feather as a series of lines: as seen by a bird as a mass of curly hair (resembling a nest).

The results of this exercise may amaze you. Most sentences created this way sound surprisingly like statements from translations of ancient Egyptian. This system was developed by the noted author and lecturer, Jean Houston.

Collecting Symbols

You can quickly compile a symbols folder if you simply scan all the "junk mail" that you receive. Before you pitch it, tear out the small drawings, logos, and symbols that appeal to you and file them. Bring your folder to class and show the students your treasures. Then, invite your class to collect their own.

Students can compile folders of symbol ideas that have been clipped from newspapers and magazines, copied from library books, and created by the students themselves. I also encourage students to share freely and copy the symbols that they see on mind maps made by other people.

When a child is stuck for an appropriate symbol, I ask the class to brainstorm as many ideas as they can. There is no one "right" symbol for a given concept or idea. Each person will develop a repertoire of symbols that work best for him or her. These may also vary among maps made by the same person.

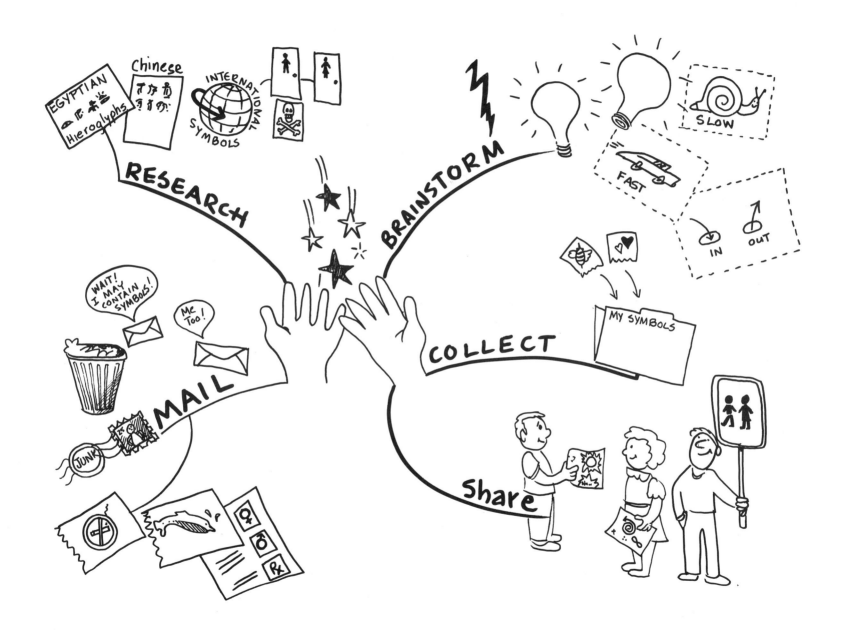

Chapter 5

Mind Mapping with Your Students

Rudolf Arnheim explored the relationship of visual images to thought. In his book, *Art and Visual Perception*, he states that for every idea, no matter how abstract, we have a corresponding visual image. The mind processes visual images with greater ease than words, Arnheim argues, because visual images precede language and are shared with our prehuman ancestors. The mind has been adapted to handle images for millions of years longer than we've had language.

Materials needed:
For each student:
    unlined paper, 11" x 17"
    colored markers or crayons
For the teacher:
    colored chalk
    unlined paper 26" x 33" (for flip chart)
    broad-tip colored markers
    markers for highlighting

Prereading

Mapping provides an excellent activity for preschoolers and older students who have not yet learned to read. First, demonstrate mind maps on a flip chart or chalkboard and then ask your students to make their own.

■ Stories can easily be built from mind maps of actual events, fantasies, or plans for future activities. The teacher might tell a story to the class and then ask each person to create a map of his or her understanding of the story.

■ Vocabulary and spelling can be taught by printing words next to symbols on the map.

■ Maps can be used to show relationships such as cause and effect or similarities. These relationships can then be used as the basis of written sentences such as, "If ___happens, then ___." Or "___and ___ are the same."

■ For teaching English as a second language, mapping provides a bridge between the two languages. Images that are easily understood can be placed on the map with the English words added as they are learned. Maps enable students to record complex relationships and events without requiring any specific grammar. After the concepts are mapped, you can assist students in writing an "English version" of their ideas.

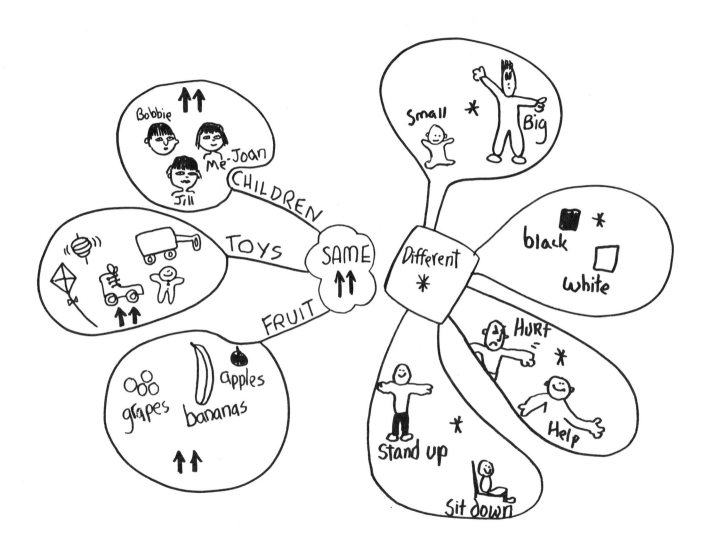

75

Learning in Context

In school settings, as in homes, one of the challenges is teaching the context as well as the concept. For example, learning a fact of history may seem rather meaningless and hard to remember unless it is seen in the larger context of historical trends, cause and effect, and so on. A mind map can place an event, or a fact from any curriculum, in context.

Memory works best when we can place new information in a context of existing information. For example, when you hear about a country that you have visited, you are more likely to remember the information because you already have a wealth of associations, memories, and impressions about that country.

Quite the opposite occurs if you hear or read a fact about a country that you know little or nothing about. There is no memory hook or anchor for this new information, and it is likely to be quickly forgotten. A mind map, like existing memories, places information in a context. Because it is in context, the information is more memorable.

Mapping Responsibilities

For practical concerns, maps can be used to establish routines and areas of responsibility. The assignment of jobs is not always met with the enthusiasm we might hope for; mind mapping can take out some of the sting.

■ Begin this process with a large sheet of paper, perhaps on the floor with everyone seated around the paper, and decide who will act as mind map scribe for the group. That person might be you, the teacher, but it works as well to give the opportunity to a child who likes to make mind maps.

■ The discussion could begin with everyone contributing ideas about what tasks need to be done on a regular basis. That would involve keeping the room neat, sending reports to the office, planning special outings, or collecting class dues.

■ The tasks are recorded first, taking care to add a few items that are fun. Color codes might help, such as red for once a week and blue for daily activities. Each person volunteers for the task he or she would like to do. You can then discuss which tasks will fall on specific days of the week. Two or three people might decide to team up on certain activities, sharing the responsibilities or taking turns.

■ Notice that on the sample map, few symbols are used. Maps do not always need to be filled with symbols. A map of tasks gives each person the context in which they, like everyone else, have jobs to do.

■ Another version of this process is to brainstorm all tasks and then highlight each student's area of responsibility with a different color.

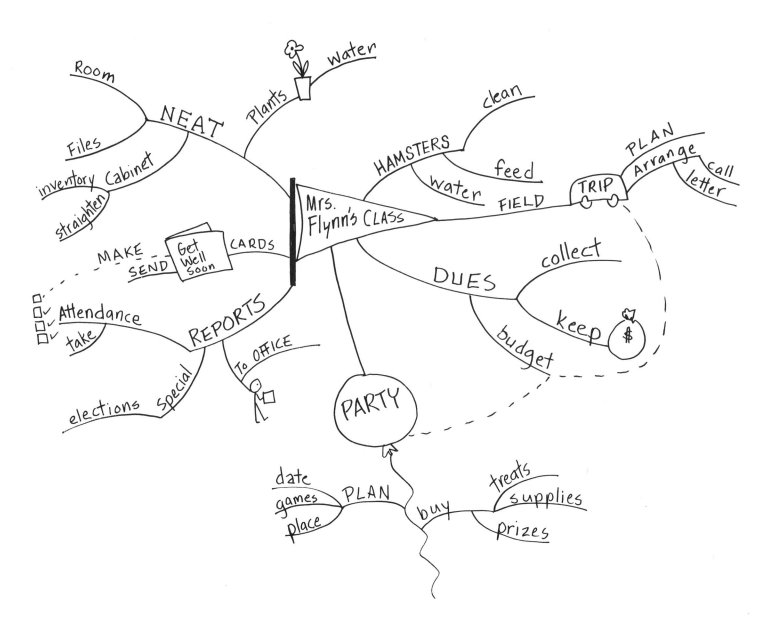

Room

NEAT

Files

inventory Cabinet

straighten

Plants — water

Mrs. Flynn's CLASS

HAMSTERS — clean

feed

water FIELD

TRIP — PLAN Arrange — call

letter

MAKE — CARDS

SEND Get Well Soon

Attendance

take

REPORTS

elections Special

To OFFICE

DUES — collect

keep $

budget

PARTY

date

games PLAN buy

place

treats

supplies

prizes

Developing a Positive Self-Image

In order to assist students to look more carefully at themselves, I suggest the following map.

▌ Begin with a central image that represents the topic: THINGS I CAN DO.

▌ From there, branch out to include anything that comes to mind. For some children, this may be only sports, for others only academic activities. I walk among the students and read aloud some of the words I see or describe the images to encourage everyone to consider the range of "Can Do's" possible.

▌ If encouragement is needed, I make a sample on the board of some of my "can do's" and include simple things like "bake cookies" and interpersonal skills such as "listen to friends." This activity provides a good opportunity to show how branching occurs from one key word.

▌ When the maps are completed, I ask everyone to add to their maps at least five things that they want to be able to do. These should be added wherever they fit on the map. Then I ask the group to tell me what things they have added, and I repeat them as if they are already an accomplished fact: *"CAN play football; CAN teach school; CAN have lots of friends."*

In this exercise teachers reinforce the notion that you are more likely to get what you want if you know what you want. It seems simple enough, but many of us never put those wishes into a concrete form by writing them down and sharing them with others. As Norman Cousins wrote, *"It is not foolish to dream of better things,...we discover ourselves as human beings when we move in the direction of our dreams."* (Cousins 1989, 68)

To emphasize this point with younger groups, I pretend to be some strange lady who wanders into the class asking for directions. *"How do I get there?"* I ask. *"Can you help me figure out how to go to get there?"*

When they ask, *"Where? Where do you want to go?"* I say, *"I don't know!"*

It becomes obvious that until I know where I want to go, there is no way to figure how to get there. If I say, *"I want to go to Chicago,"* we can figure out many ways that I can travel there. The same is true of life, and I encourage children and adults alike to make frequent maps to help them figure out where they want to go and what they want to be able to do, have, and be.

Improving Study Skills

Even though older students may need to read a book that has been assigned, there is still great benefit in looking over the entire book first.

▌ Tell students to read titles, summaries, charts, maps, and the index where many pages are noted for important topics.

▌ After skimming the main segments of the book,

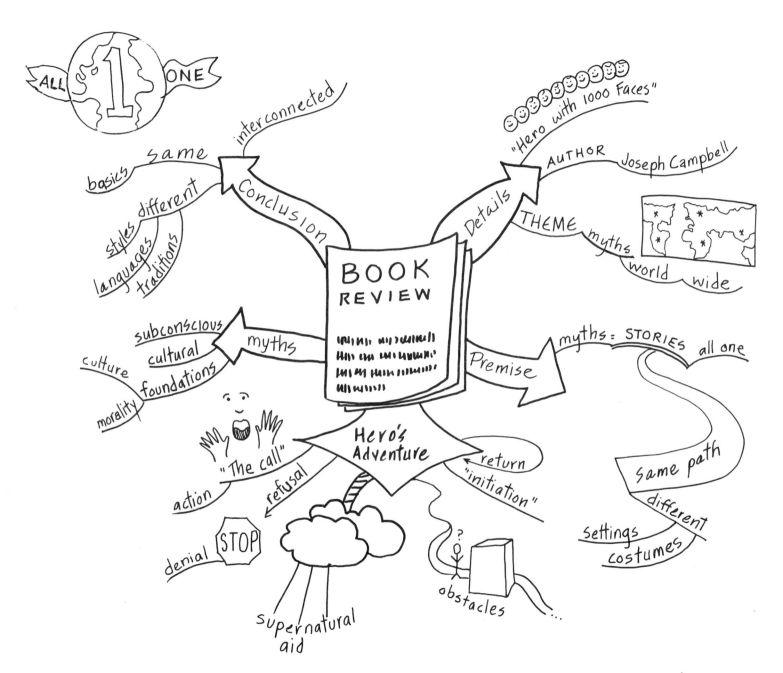

ALL **1** ONE

interconnected

basics same
styles different
languages traditions

Conclusion

"Hero with 1000 Faces"
AUTHOR Joseph Campbell
Details THEME myths world wide

BOOK REVIEW

subconscious
culture cultural
morality foundations

myths

Premise

myths= STORIES all one

Same path
settings different
costumes

"The call"
action refusal
denial STOP

Hero's Adventure

return "initiation"

supernatural aid

obstacles ?
...

students should then make a skeleton map of the key topics. Making an overview map gives a sense of the whole or context into which details of the book fit.

∎ After creating a skeletal map, the student then reads the book, or selected parts of the book, adding to the map any fact or concept that he or she wants to remember.

The map on page 79 was created by Steven Kowalsky.

For students, making mind map notes from books is a way of representing their individual "knowing." They are representing on paper their own unique structure for the ideas in the book, which requires a higher-order thinking process than just underlining key points. Mapping becomes, in effect, teaching the habit of *thinking while learning.* Adding one's own understanding and structure to the topic requires active participation in the learning process.

Expanding Thinking Skills

One of the greatest problems facing educators today is that of the passive learner. Television as well as traditional teaching methods have created a tendency in students to sit back in the classroom with the same energy level they bring to sitting in front of a television set. The expectation that many children bring to school is that they can sit back and be entertained and at the same time wonder what the sponsor is trying to pawn off on them.

Asking that students create notes in mind map form requires that they do more than write down selected phrases from a book or lecture. Mapping reflects the learner's understanding of concepts and relationships and, at its best, requires active thinking about the subject being recorded.

I recommend that you enhance this aspect of mapping with assignments such as:

∎ Make two maps of the subject, each with a different central image. For example, if you are studying a short story in a literature class, map the story with the focus on a specific character, and then map it again with a particular setting, mood, theme, action, or event as your central image.

∎ Map the subject you are studying in pictures only.

∎ Map only the relationships in a story or subject. For example, map the influences, impacts, and trends related to a certain historical event.

∎ Create a map and then walk another student through your map, explaining each element of your map.

∎ Read a story, make a map from it, and then give your map to another student, without telling the name of your story or discussing it. The other student then reads your map and from it writes his or her idea of what the story might be about.

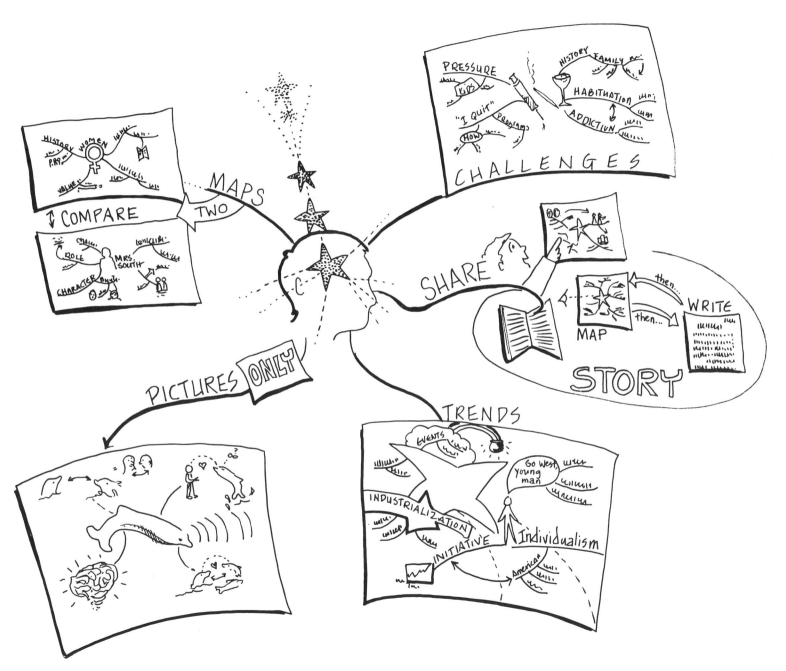

MAPS

TWO

HISTORY WOMEN
PRG
VALUE

COMPARE

ROLE
MRS. SOUTH
CHARACTER

PRESSURE
KIDS
"I QUIT" Programs
HOW

HISTORY FAMILY
HABITUATION
ADDICTION

CHALLENGES

SHARE

then...
then...
MAP
WRITE

STORY

PICTURES ONLY

TRENDS

EVENTS

Go West
young
man

INDUSTRIALIZATION
INITIATIVE Individualism
American

■ Ask students to map plans for a field trip. After the trip, map what actually occurred.

■ Ask older students to map situations that they find difficult to manage such as moving to a new school or dealing with the presence of drugs or alcohol at a party. Each person can add coping strategies to the maps as ideas are shared in small-group discussions.

Brainstorming

Mind mapping fits perfectly as the written component of brainstorming. Brainstorming has proved to be a most effective method for generating creative ideas and for problem solving in corporate settings as well as classrooms. Brainstorming is also effective in meetings of professionals including faculty groups and curriculum planners.

The more ideas you generate, the more ideas from which you can choose. The synergy developed through positive group process is one that all students should be exposed to.

When brainstorming in a group, try the following guidelines:

▶ Ask one person to mind map at the board or at an easel for the group.

▶ Accept all ideas, even if they appear unlikely, odd, or impossible.

▶ Do not judge the ideas.

▶ Don't discuss why ideas might not work.

▶ Piggyback one idea on another.

This system is excellent for seeing the ideas of a group emerge and encouraging participation by all members of a class. You can model the mapping system by recording students' ideas as they are presented. The result, a group mind map, can then be posted where students can add their ideas as they occur or make their own maps of the ideas they like best from the brainstorming session.

Mapping in High School

Michael Gelb once presented a three-day workshop for the sophomore class of Paint Branch High School in Maryland. The students were assigned to read and report on a history textbook, using the study skills Gelb had taught them. One student who didn't like school and didn't like to do assignments, refused to read a book and report on it to the members of his group.

Gelb told him, *"OK. Don't read the book. Just make a mind map from the table of contents and use the map as the basis for your report to your group."*

The student made his map and became very involved in the project. He found that he could enjoy learning, could convey his ideas on paper, and gave one of the the best reports in the class.

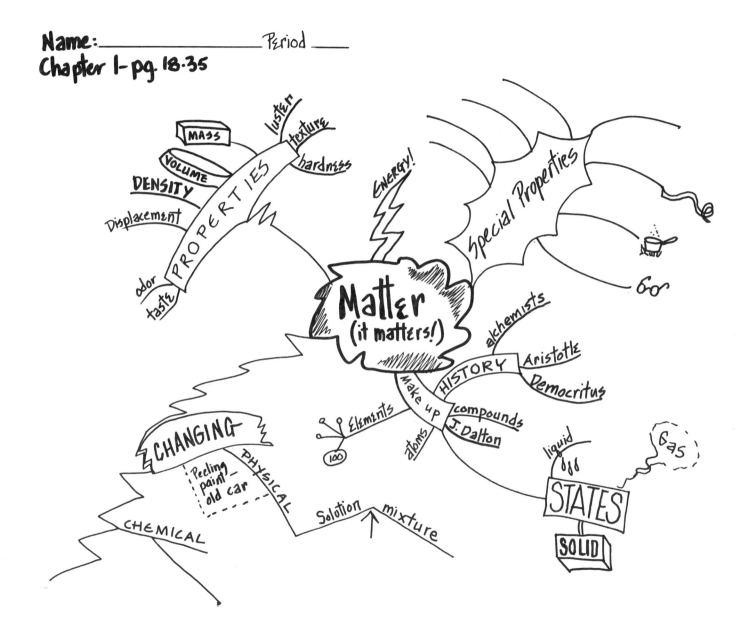

Matter
(it matters!)

PROPERTIES
MASS
VOLUME
DENSITY
luster
texture
hardness
Displacement
odor
taste

ENERGY!

Special Properties

600

HISTORY
alchemists
Aristotle
Democritus

Make up
Elements
100
atoms
compounds
J. Dalton

STATES
liquid
Gas
SOLID

CHANGING
PHYSICAL
Peeling paint - old car
CHEMICAL
Solution
mixture

Pat Dalton, a high school science teacher in St. Louis, created the map on the previous page for her students to add to as they studied "Matter."

She also uses mind maps with her biology classes and comments on her first experience:

"I wasn't very sophisticated about it — in fact I had just learned to map the day before I introduced the concept to my classes, but it went very well. I teach three classes in a row of the same subject, which is true for many teachers at the high school level.

In the first class I introduced the basic terms we would be using as we studied animal classifications. I told the group we were going to try a new system — mind mapping — and for that we would need symbols. I asked them to work with me to develop little drawings to represent such categories as "soft-bodied creatures" and "mollusks." We had fun coming up with ideas. I especially liked the fish and person in a file drawer to represent the fact that humans and fish are in the same phylum.

Once we had our basic symbols on the board, everyone copied them, and we had a map of biological classifications.

The next group came in and, rather than erasing the board and beginning all over again, I decided to show them the symbols the class before them had just created. In doing so, I explained each classification, and we moved on from there. That second-hour class got further in the material than the first and had time to invent new symbols for the next lesson.

The third class had the benefit of the first two, moved along rapidly through the material, and made up symbols for the last section of the unit.

The next day I showed the first group what the other two had invented, and we were off and running. Now the benefit of this, aside from the fact that it was fun, is that when I tested my students on the material I was amazed at how much they remembered. I tried traditional tests on the first two groups, and then for my third hour class, I used mind mapping as a part of the test. To accomplish that, I showed them a map I had made of the symbols, and asked them to select two branches of the map and write an essay about them. Again, the recall of the material was very impressive."

In the mind map on page 85, a student in another class created novel symbols for chordates.

Bernice Bleedorn, the Director for Creative Studies at the College of St. Thomas in St. Paul, Minnesota, has been using mind mapping with her students since she

= Vertebrates

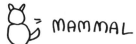
= MAMMAL

= REPTILES

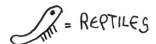
= BIRDS

amphibians

FISH
BONY Fish

JAWLESS Fish

Cartilage fish

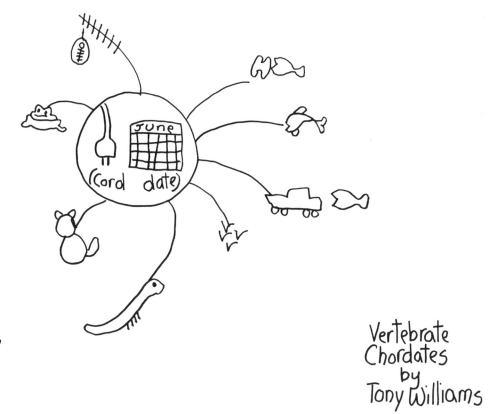

June

(cord date)

Vertebrate
Chordates
by
Tony Williams

first learned the technique in the early '80s. Her approach can be used with high school students as well as at the college level.

"I have made extensive use of mapping for generating ideas and planning the writing of papers and articles for publication, as well as planning talks and seminars. Mapping has become the 'first line of attack' for just about any substantial communication. More specifically, I am constantly promoting mapping in my classes. I require the presentation of a book review on a book relevant to the course content, chosen by the student, read, and mapped for the class. Maps are brought to class, and the presentations are made from the maps rather than from a complex set of notes or formal paper. I make a strong case for 'whole brain thinking,' with mapping an aid to balancing spontaneous, systematic, visual thinking and communicating with traditional sequential, verbal systems.

Mind mapping as a strategy has been transferring successfully to other educational settings. Teachers who have been in my Creative Studies class...report that when they introduce the concept of mapping and encourage it as an alternative language, students in elementary grades who have been relatively constrained in their writing assignments begin to express complex thinking patterns through the creation of a map. New thinking 'stars' are discovered when alternative communication systems are introduced.

Students from my undergraduate course on Entrepreneurial Creative Thinking and Problem Solving develop some extremely effective maps, and book reviews presented from maps take on a particularly energetic and articulate style. It becomes clear that students have really internalized the reading material and understand it as a system."

The map on page 87 is based on a student map which could be used for a presentation to the class, adding words and symbols to the top of the map as they are introduced.

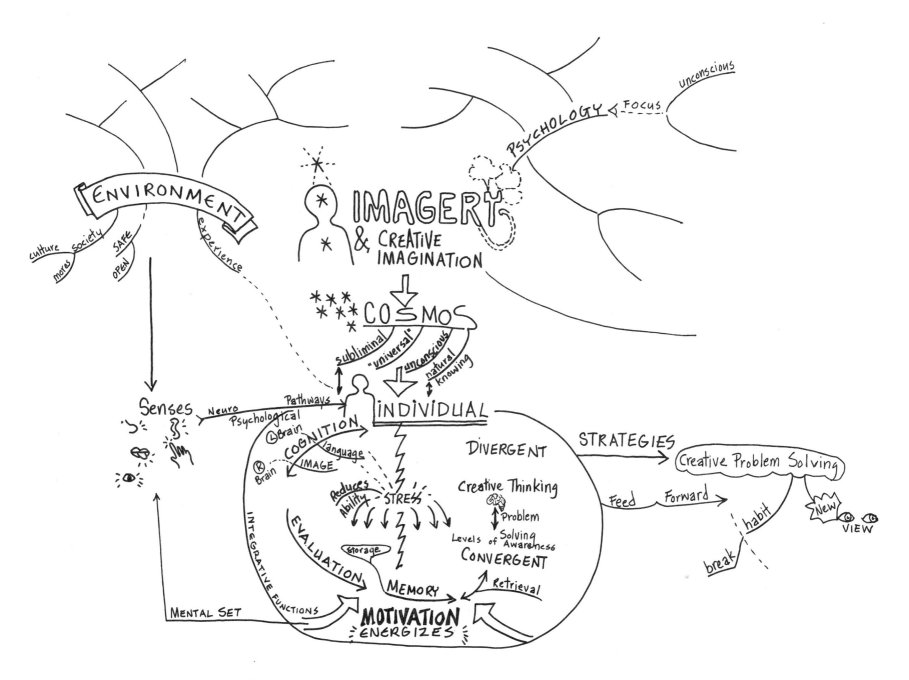

ENVIRONMENT

culture   society
mores   SAFE
OPEN
experience

IMAGERY
& CREATIVE
IMAGINATION

PSYCHOLOGY   FOCUS   unconscious

COSMOS

subliminal   "universal"   unconscious   natural knowing

Senses   Neuro   Pathways
Psychological   Brain

INDIVIDUAL

COGNITION
language
L Brain
IMAGE
R Brain

DIVERGENT

STRATEGIES

Creative Problem Solving

Creative Thinking

Reduces
Ability   STRESS

Problem
Solving
Levels of Awareness
CONVERGENT

Feed   Forward

NEW
VIEW
break   habit

EVALUATION

storage

MEMORY   Retrieval

INTEGRATIVE FUNCTIONS

MENTAL SET

MOTIVATION
ENERGIZES

Chapter 6

Mapping with Others

Parents and Children

The fact that mapping is an easy tool to learn makes it ideal for parents to teach their children. Mapping can be a creative and functional tool for families to use together. As a result, mapping does not have to feel like "homework" but can be "homeplay!" Families use mapping for planning vacations, negotiating differences, recording things to do around the house, and sharing ideas.

This concept can be applied to explaining rules in a family or social context. If you prepare a simple map using pictures wherever possible, you can then walk a young child through the map and explain each element as you do so. You are giving the child the context in which to understand and better remember the information.

Young children can be introduced to mapping in the same order that they acquire a language. That is, they take it in and see it in use before they are expected to produce it themselves. In this model the child is intro-

duced to maps that the parents, older siblings, or teachers make and explain, mind map notes that parents leave them (as in the facing sample), or other special maps that are made expressly for them, such as one that captures a favorite story.

Children Who Have Hearing Impairments

This section is intended for teachers of children who are deaf and for educators interested in this field, but generally unfamiliar with deafness. Many of the techniques described here can also be applied to children with language delays, learning disabilities, or other problems related to their ability to process language.

For the purposes of this chapter, I will focus on children who have a hearing loss acquired at an early age, a loss so great that language must be received through the eyes, not the ears. This group is referred to as prelingually, profoundly deaf. Those who are hearing impaired but can understand speech through auditory channels, are not included in this definition, although they certainly can benefit, like the rest of us, from mind mapping.

In the United States an enormous variety of teaching methods are used to educate children who are deaf. The children and adults I have worked with, like most profoundly deaf people, use American Sign Language (ASL), which, although a complete language, does not conform to English syntax. A person may be fluent in

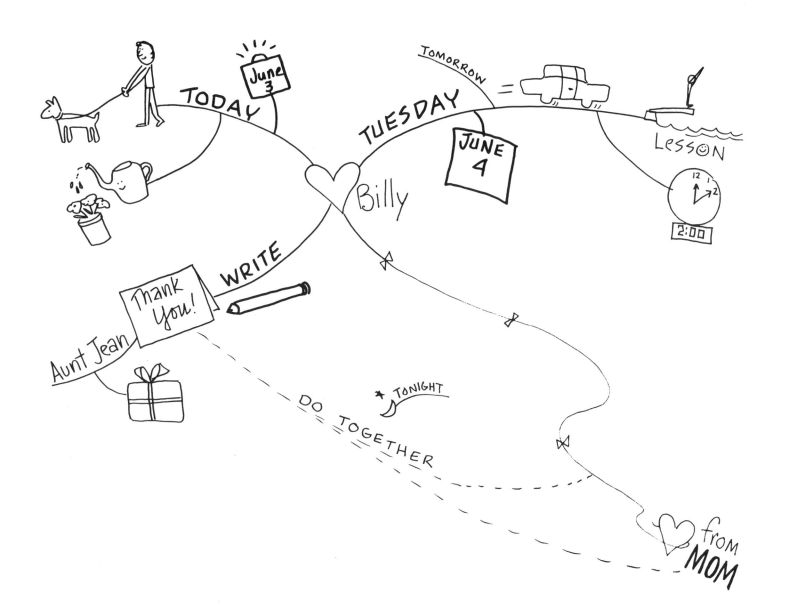

89

American Sign Language, even eloquent, poetic, and dramatic, yet still experience enormous difficulty writing ideas in English.

While ASL has more dimensions to it that any spoken language, it has no written component. As a result, many deaf children do not use paper and pencil to record their ideas or develop strategies. Certainly a shopping list can be written, but the more complex and wide-ranging benefits of writing ideas on paper has been the province of those who are literate in the written form of a spoken language.

However, mind mapping provides a method for recording ideas that does not require English grammar. It requires some key words, symbols, use of space and color, and a comfort with visually representing ideas. For these visual tasks, people who are deaf are generally better qualified than most of their hearing counterparts (Sacks 1989). Mapping is not by any means a written sign language, but it can provide children who are deaf with the many benefits of writing their ideas on paper. Most importantly, it is a visual system and as such is well suited to those who use ASL and are acknowledged visual experts.

As Hughlings-Jackson states, *"We speak not only to tell other people what we think, but to tell ourselves what we think. Speech is part of thought."* For those who use a visual language, sign is part of thought. When mapping, we create a visual image of our thoughts so that we can "see what we are thinking." This benefit is certainly not limited to children who have hearing impairments. (Many people tell me that they find themselves making maps to "find out what they are thinking!" Try mapping when you are feeling confused or confronting a dilemma which you seemingly cannot resolve. Often the answer will appear on the map.)

Mind mapping can be introduced to children who are deaf by teachers or parents, adapting the techniques introduced in earlier chapters. Maps take advantage of the love of drawing which I have found to be particularly strong in those who have hearing impairments. Regardless of how they are being educated, these children need to take in language visually. Mind mapping, precisely because it is a visual language, is similar to sign language in its emphasis upon spatial relations, concepts, icons, pictures, and nonlinear representation. Beyond that, the system can be used to foster an understanding of the context in which an event occurs — a concept that is often difficult to convey.

Of course we know that people who are deaf miss a great deal because they can't hear what is being said to them. What we often fail to realize is that they miss even more because they don't *over*hear anything either. Overhearing, which is part of incidental learning, enables us to pick up much of the information that we need to develop and mature. Your parents may never have sat you down for lessons in conflict resolution, but you

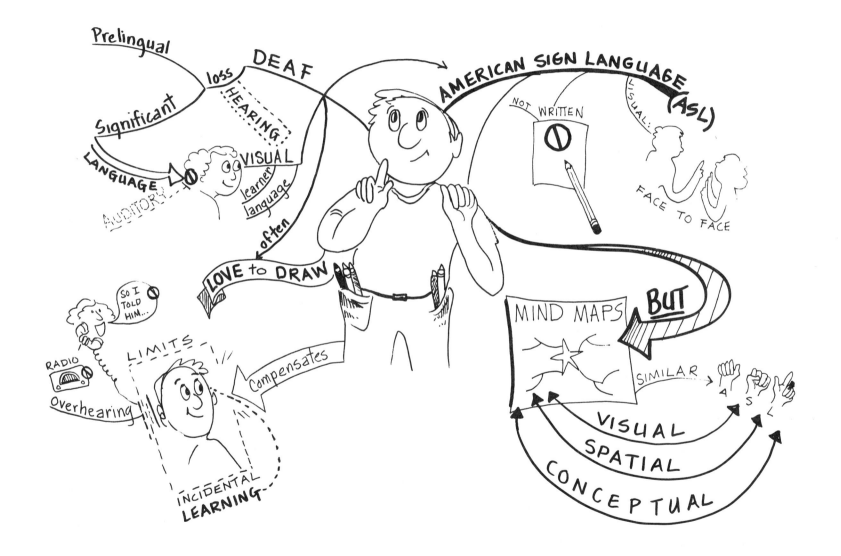

Prelingual

Significant

LANGUAGE

AUDITORY

loss

DEAF

HEARING

VISUAL
learner
language

often

VISUAL

LOVE to DRAW

AMERICAN SIGN LANGUAGE (ASL)

NOT WRITTEN

VISUAL:

FACE TO FACE

SO I TOLD HIM...

RADIO

Overhearing

LIMITS

Compensates

INCIDENTAL LEARNING

MIND MAPS

BUT

SIMILAR

ASL

VISUAL

SPATIAL

CONCEPTUAL

91

learned a great deal by hearing them talk to each other at home or to friends on the telephone. Radio, television, movies, and conversations that took place all around you from infancy on are a vital part of your informal education.

For the child who is deaf, we need methods that compensate for the loss of this vital incidental learning. When a child uses mapping, and the adults in his or her world use maps, too, there is more opportunity to explore and explain ideas. This is not meant to replace other forms of communication, but rather to enhance and expand them.

As a psychologist working with deaf children, I noticed that many of my clients were not aware of the range of choices available to them in most situations. They tended to wait for the world to have an impact upon them, rather than take an active stance to make things happen.

▮ Mapping the myriad of choices available, mapping a plan of what you want and how you might go about achieving your goals, has proved to be extremely useful. Maps can be used to emphasize that in any given situation many choices do exist. One can begin by generating a multitude of possible options and then narrowing the field and making a selection.

Other topics for maps that work well with children who are deaf include:

▶ What I can do. Encourage the student to list simple everyday accomplishments as well as more complex skills. This exercise contributes to a positive self-image, and the habit of acknowledging even the small successes. Too often the emphasis for a child with deafness is the limitation rather than the strength.

▶ What I want to be able to do. This can be added as phase two on the CAN DO map, or be made separately. Projecting into the future and clearly stating goals serve to encourage students to focus upon their own potential and create a greater sense of direction for their activities and studies.

▶ What is most important in my life.

▶ What I know about (any topic they have been studying in school).

▶ Theme maps such as one on peace help clarify ideas of the topic. Deafness often contributes to highly individual world views, virtually untouched by influences such as television. Therefore, when we say or sign "peace" or any other general term, it is important to know how that is understood by the student who is deaf.

▮ In addition to teaching the children to generate maps of their own, use maps that you create to show the overview of a topic they are studying, to explain relationships of persons in the family, and to map out the plans for the coming week.

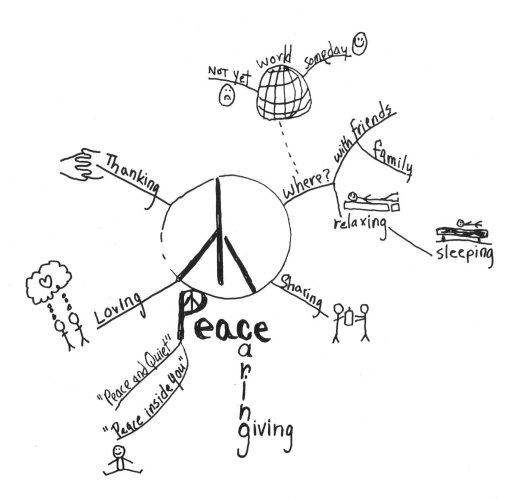

by Evan Howard

In order to encourage the child to make decisions, you can map the acceptable alternatives or plans and let the child select the one you will do, or what you will do first.

A map of upcoming events provides an excellent way to convey to the child what will be happening during the coming week. The ability to anticipate events, as well as to participate in making plans, is an important one that is often delayed or absent in deaf children. In many cases, full communication is lacking between the deaf child and his or her family. When this happens, the child is left out of the decision-making process and does not understand the process of planning, anticipating, and acting assertively. The map activities will serve as one of the tools available to you to remedy this situation.

Maps can also be used to study English. Try a map that shows all the possible meanings for a word such as "run." The map might include symbols or sketches of meanings in phrases such as "a run on apples" - "a run in her stocking" - "a home run" - "run out of money"- "run for office" — you know, English IS a confusing language!

Barbara Doyle, an innovative teacher of deaf children from Illinois, was using mind maps before she had ever heard the term.

"I mapped all sorts of relationships with the children," she reports.

"For example, we made maps that showed processes that are not readily apparent, such as 'where milk comes from.' We began with a cow in the field and ended up with a picture of milk on the table. Maps were extremely helpful, too, when planning a community activity, such as a visit to the zoo or a trip to the store. I mapped the event in advance with the children, and then we discussed possible areas where communication could be a problem. We planned augmentations such as having a card prepared with your order for McDonald's or studying the guidelines to checking out a book in the library in advance of the trip."

Special Learners

Many students are not naturally sequential in the way they learn and interpret the world. Because we have tended to teach with an emphasis upon the sequential, these children have been labeled "Learning Disabled."

Although there is no doubt that the range of abilities among children is great, we could use the term "Teaching Disabled" to describe the way that we have failed to reach many children. For those children with obvious difficulty learning and storing material in a sequential manner, we can offer the "patterning" of mind maps. Many bright "stars" will be uncovered when the opportunity to create individual maps is introduced. This will give the children who may not stand out as exceptionally able an opportunity to lead the class.

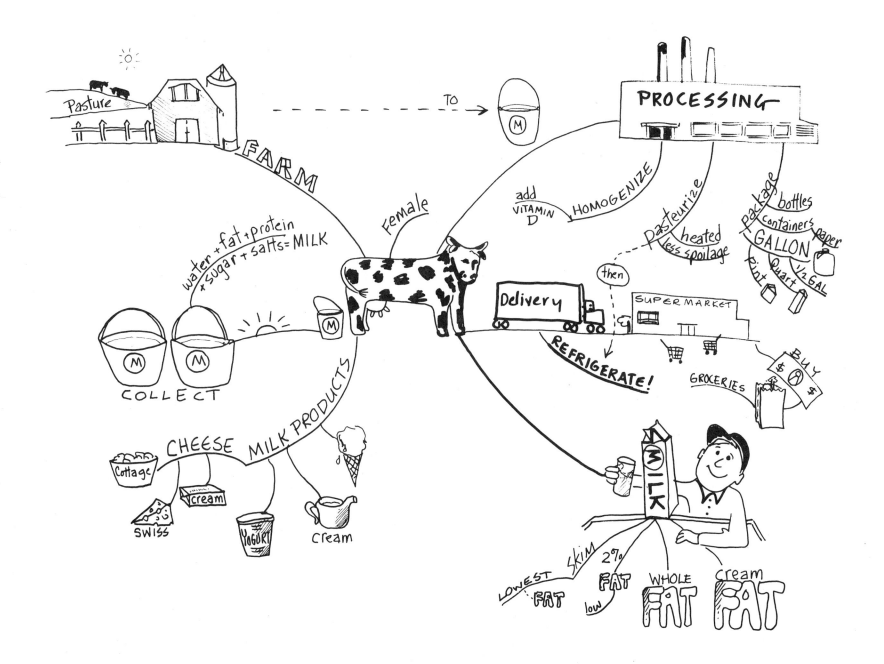

Judy Golde, a third grade teacher, uses mapping with students who cannot read. First the student, encouraged to use symbols, creates a map of a story, then using the map as a guide, explains the story to a small group. Next, the teacher, a teacher's aide or a fellow student who likes to write, records the story. The student then practices reading, using a story of his or her own creation. The map serves to show both the overview of the story and the way in which the details fit together to create the whole.

OVERVIEW

details

FIT!

5 MAP

illustration
reminder

Judy's IDEA

STUDENT
reading
writing   difficult

1

STORY

MAP
Pictures

2

4 PRACTICE

Reading

TELL

RECORD   student
assistant -or- older

3

MAP

STORY

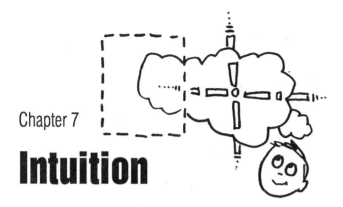

Chapter 7

Intuition

One aspect of human intelligence that places us above the animals and the computers is intuition. Strongly linked with creativity, intuition can be developed in everyone. Willis Harmon, president of the Institute of Noetic Sciences, says that the only real barrier to using our intuition fully is our own limiting beliefs. Most of us don't want to put too much faith in our intuitive senses and have trouble giving credit when our "hunches" turn out to be accurate. Aldous Huxley wrote that cognitive and receptive intuitive powers can be developed. *"Both kinds of training are absolutely indispensable. If you neglect either, you'll never grow into a fully human being."* (Huxley 1962)

I assume that you are a person open to new ideas (you are, after all, reading a book on mind mapping at this very minute!) and that you believe that the development of intuition can be useful, if not critical, to us in the future. In that case, how do we foster intuition in children as well as in ourselves? In order to look at that question, let us first define some of the aspects of the intuitive process.

Intuitive experiences:

▶ often occur when we are in relaxed situations and not "working at" anything

▶ are frequently symbolic in nature and cannot easily be expressed in words

▶ often involve seeing new connections occur spontaneously, seemingly out of the blue

The first step in developing intuition is to believe that it is possible. I ask my students not to adopt my belief, but to *pretend* it is true that we all possess unlimited abilities to tap our inner knowing.

Mapping Inner Knowing with Students

Ask your class to pretend that they have access to information through their intuitive powers. These powers could be given a name such as "the source of knowing," a "wise guide," or a "spirit of knowledge." To further the realization process, play relaxing music while each person sits comfortably in front of a paper on which they will map their ideas. Guide them as follows:

"Sit comfortably, with your arms and legs uncrossed...Let your eyes slowly close...Become aware of your breathing...As you breathe in, imagine that you are being filled with light, and

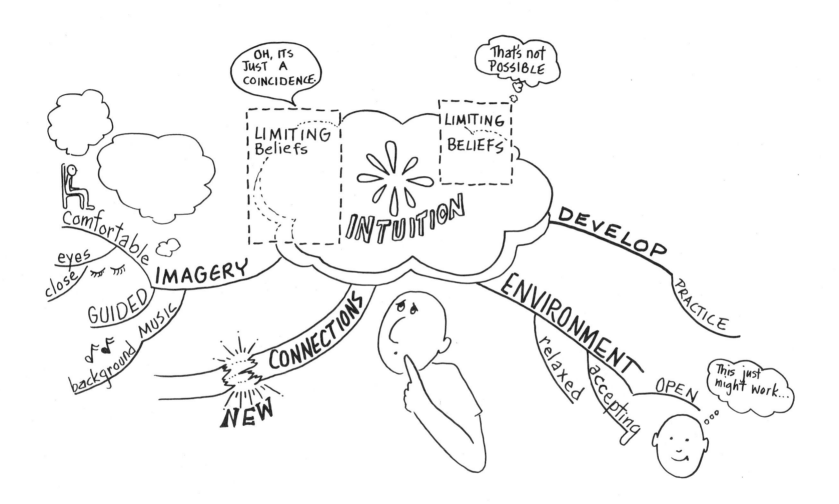

as you breathe out, let all the tension flow from you. Each time you breathe out, you can feel yourself relax more and more...Imagine that you are floating on a blue cloud, comfortable and happy. Your body is becoming relaxed, and you can feel the tension going out from your feet all the way to the top of your head...You will open your eyes in a minute, but the calm feeling will stay with you."

At this point ask your students to slowly open their eyes. Then pose a question. Remind your class that there are no right or wrong answers here and that they will not be asked to show their intuition maps to another person.

Your question may be one that you select or one that the class has agreed upon in advance. The question can be a genuine problem that everyone is experiencing, a challenge facing our country or world, a question about the unknown beyond space and time, beyond the world we see and experience. Some of the questions that I have found most provocative of intuitive answers include:

▶ What will our world be like in the future?

▶ What are the most important things in life?

▶ What can I do to make my life better right now?

▶ Is there life in outer space?

▶ What can our school do about the drug problem?

▶ What are the best ways to make and keep friends?

▶ What do my parents really want for me?

When ready, each person draws a symbol of inner knowing anywhere on the page. Students should follow their hunches and do whatever occurs to them. Any words or images that occur to them should be recorded without judging their worth.

While mapping, the students should not feel limited by guidelines such as one word per line, connect each line, or radiate from the central image. Instead, let the associations, thoughts, and ideas flow freely. Any idea, no matter how seemingly strange, should be included. If words don't occur to them, students can try pictures, symbols, or colors. There is no need to understand what students are recording; they just let it happen.

In this activity, many students will be launched on an intuitive journey. Others may need more encouragement. In those cases, it's helpful to explain that each of us has an "internal judge" who looks at our actions or ideas and says things like "that's dumb" or "you're weird." For this map, draw a little judge or an image that represents him or her in a corner of the map; then put a big "X" or a red circle with a slash through it over the judge. Urge students to let their hand and marker be directed by their own impulses and to ignore the judge.

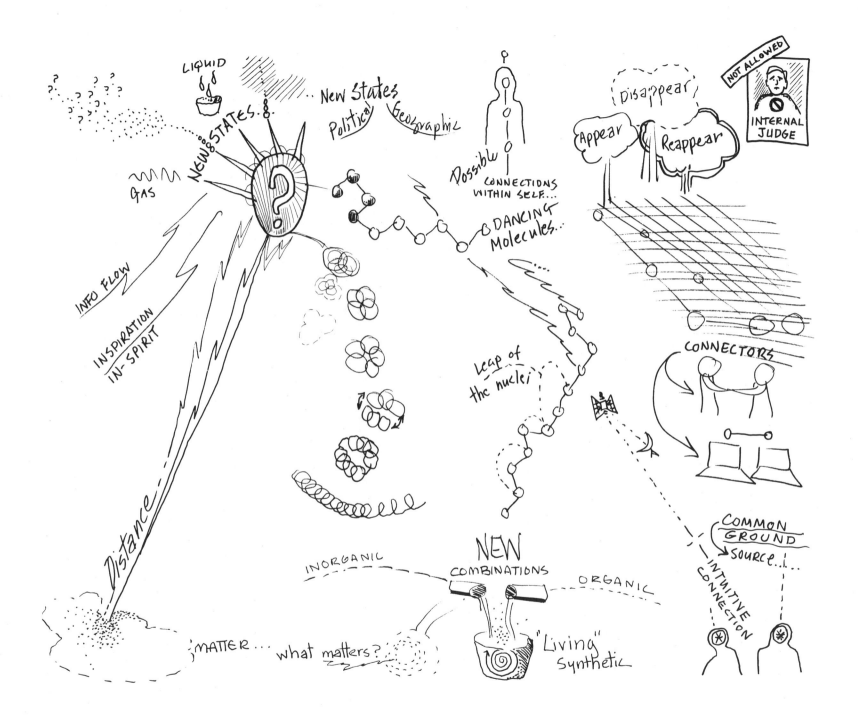

LIQUID

NEW STATES

New States
Political Geographic

GAS

INFO FLOW

INSPIRATION
IN-SPIRIT

Distance

Possible
CONNECTIONS
WITHIN SELF...

DANCING
Molecules...

Leap of
the nuclei

Disappear
Appear   Reappear

NOT ALLOWED
INTERNAL
JUDGE

CONNECTORS

COMMON
GROUND
SOURCE...

INTUITIVE
CONNECTION

INORGANIC

NEW
COMBINATIONS

ORGANIC

MATTER... what matters?

"Living"
Synthetic

101

You can also assist students by adding to the guided relaxation more specific images such as the following:

"You are feeling deeply relaxed now. You are floating on a blue cloud over a beautiful valley full of flowers. The cloud moves down into the valley until you are sitting among the flowers. You can smell the lovely scent of the flowers and feel the warmth of the sun on your face. Then you notice someone walking toward you. You can't see who it is, but you have a feeling that the person is good, kind, and very, very wise. This is a person who can answer any question.

As the person comes closer, you stand up and soon the two of you are face to face. You look into each other's eyes and smile. You have a question in your mind ... think of that question ... and now you ask the question to this wise person. The wise person says 'I will guide you. I will help you find the answer to your question. I will help you find the information you need. When you are ready to ask again, the answers will appear.'...

Now you are ready to say good-bye to the wise person. First you say 'thank you.' Then you turn and sit on the blue cloud that is waiting to carry you back. You float back out of the magic valley. You float back to this room where you can feel yourself sitting in your chair again. You notice your breathing in and out. I will count to ten. When I am finished, you can open your eyes, wiggle your fingers, stretch, and bring your awareness fully back into this room. 1 ... 2 ... 3 ... 4 ... 5 ... 6 ... 7 ... 8 ... 9 ... 10."

Next instruct the students to remain relaxed, not talking, but just listening to the music and mapping the answers that come to them. After allowing students to work at a comfortable pace for about ten minutes, ask them to conclude the section they are working on and take a look at what they have produced thus far. If new ideas occur to the students, they should record them on their maps.

If anyone had an experience that he or she wants to share, allow time for that. If you have tackled a more immediate and concrete problem such as, "Where is Susan's lost backpack?" then you may want to share or record the answers and see if you can track down the lost item.

Another variation of the guided imagery is to ask the students to imagine that the wise person is at the top of a very tall mountain. To ask for his or her help, they must climb the mountain. After you ask them again to relax, lead them step-by-step up a steep slope. Add as much detail as you can about what they feel, hear, smell, and see as they scale the mountain. Tell your students that at the top of the mountain, they will hear the an-

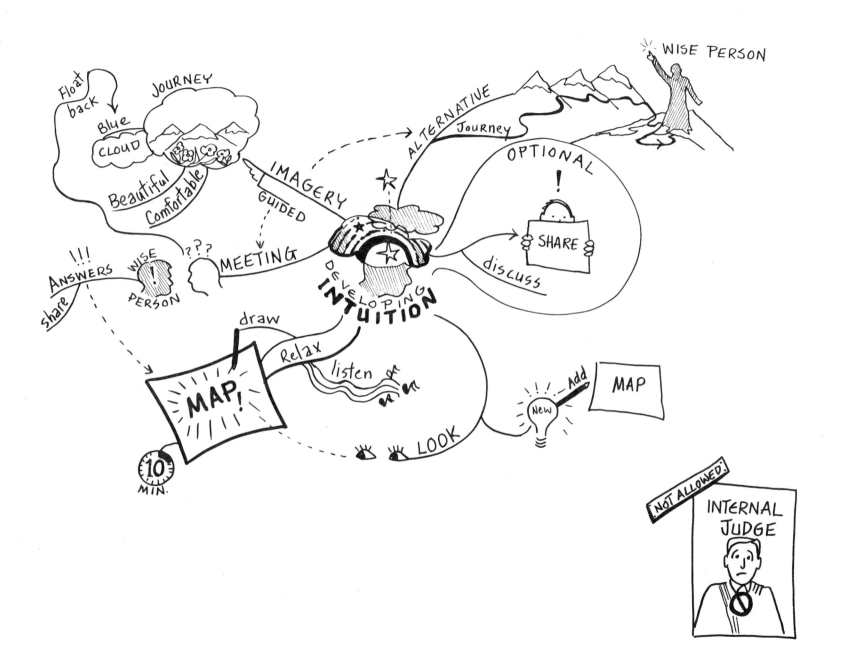

Float back

JOURNEY

Blue
CLOUD

Beautiful
Comfortable

IMAGERY

GUIDED

ALTERNATIVE
Journey

WISE PERSON

OPTIONAL
!
SHARE

DEVELOPING INTUITION

discuss

!!!
Answers
share

???

WISE PERSON

MEETING

draw

Relax

listen

MAP!

10 MIN.

LOOK

New
Add

MAP

NOT ALLOWED.

INTERNAL JUDGE

swer or receive a gift that represents the answer. Then lead them back (more rapidly this time — magic carpets are handy for this) and ask them to map the answer they received.

Intuitive Mapping

One important aspect of intuitive and creative leaps is that they often occur after much hard work and research on a given topic. The best examples of this come from science. Often a scientist works on a problem for years before suddenly having the "aha!" experience of an intuitive leap. Solving the problem in this manner is the result of gathering information and allowing creative insights to uncover new ways of putting the information together.

■ To experience this phenomenon, I suggest that you challenge your class to make an intuition map on a subject that they have not yet studied. For instance, you might select a topic in social studies, history, or science.

■ After students map their best ideas, insights, and intuition on the topic, ask them to put their maps aside. Then proceed with the unit in which they will study the topic in depth.

■ After the class has had time to learn more about the subject, to gather and think about the information available to them, ask your students to make a new map on the same topic as the first, with the same directions.

Comparing the two maps will give students a valuable lesson in the necessity of using intuition with acquired knowledge.

Perception and intuition occur through pattern recognition. *"Intuition discerns, detects, discovers patterns, forms relationships, properties, and meanings. Intuition helps you see through the facts, around the facts, into the facts, and beyond the facts."* (Barrett 1989). It is the pattern that we are developing when we create a nonlinear record of ideas in mind map form.

"And now for the next step in examining intuition. We can now talk about the mind's eye, *a common phrase, and an important one for creativity and innovation ... we can work with* images, *we can* image *things, we can* image-ine *them."* (Barrett 1989)

The map on page 105 summarizes the information on this page and also demonstrates that a map can be mostly words.

To focus on our inner images and train ourselves further in the skill of imagination, we can make maps that have no set agenda and are purely the wonderings of the mind.

■ Start with a large sheet of paper, play relaxing music, and draw whatever comes to you. Begin with a question, if you want, and see what answers appear.

■ Or begin with an image and just "doodle" your way into the language of your intuitive self.

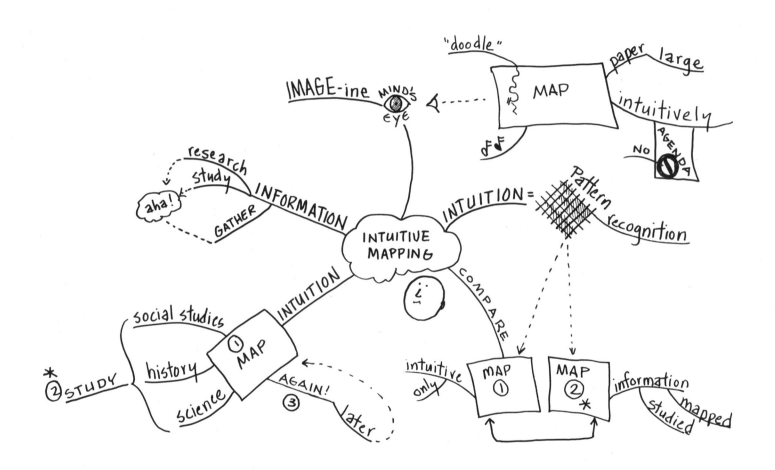

"doodle"

IMAGE-ine MIND'S EYE

paper large

MAP

intuitively

of ♪

NO AGENDA

research

study

aha!

GATHER INFORMATION

INTUITION = Pattern recognition

INTUITIVE MAPPING

COMPARE

INTUITION

social studies

① MAP

history

② STUDY

science

AGAIN!

③ later

intuitive only

MAP ①

MAP ② *

information mapped studied

Michael Gelb, the president of High Performance Learning, has coined the term Super Logic to explain what we call an intuitive leap. If you study an intuitive insight carefully, working from the "aha" backwards, you will find a logical progression. The process that brings us to intuitive knowing is extremely fast-paced and works beyond the level of verbal processing. We don't consciously know how we arrive at these insights because Super Logic is operating outside the realm of our conscious thought.

Chapter 8

Ways of Knowing

For You, the Teacher

In this chapter I will walk you step-by-step through the process of making a map of concepts. The concepts that I have selected are valuable to both educators and parents. For those of you who are already familiar with the ideas, seeing them mapped may suggest new insights or applications.

Often I attend conferences, not only to teach mind mapping, but to create mind maps while others are presenting. These maps are posted around the room and serve as a point for review and discussion of the material that is presented. As a result of my work, I have the pleasure of meeting and working with an amazing group of educators. One of the most fascinating is Parker Palmer, an educator and theologian who is the author of *To Know As We Are Known*.

The map on the opposite page was created during one of Palmer's presentations to faculty and administrators from undergraduate programs throughout the country. The map serves as a sample map, but more importantly, the content touches upon some key issues facing educators today.

Palmer believes that the role of education is to create an environment in which truth is practiced. He defines truth as an ongoing conversation about things that matter. This conversation can be between two or more persons, or it may be an internal conversation. There is no fixed, eternal, or constant truth, Palmer explains. Truth is a process and depends upon the person or persons who are experiencing and examining it.

Suppose that I want to take just that much of Parker Palmer's ideas and explore how they apply to mind mapping.

∎ To examine these relationships, I could create a map of Palmer's ideas. In the center of a page, I can draw or paste a picture of Palmer. Then, after creating several branches, I can think about how each branch might relate to mind mapping.

∎ I can then study the map to find similarities between mind mapping and Palmer's ideas.

∎ The notion that truth is a process without a specific endpoint is true of mapping, too. I place a star by PROCESS and make a key on the map to show that star will represent "true of mind mapping." Another star is added next to the symbol for conversation. Whether internal or external, conversation is communication through language, and mind mapping is as well.

Now I might begin to wonder if the points I am

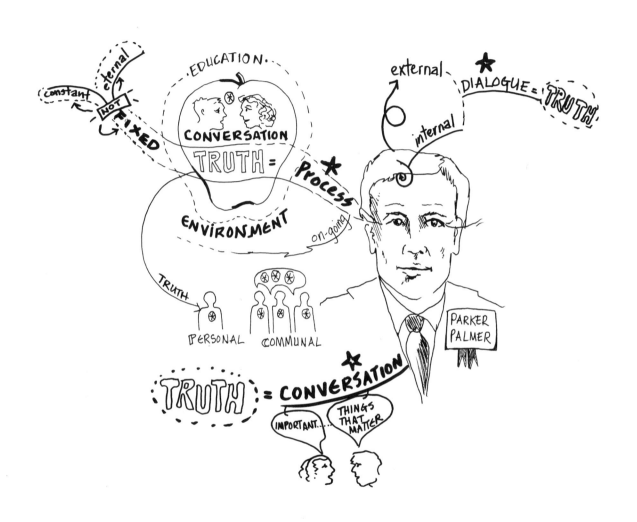

* = true of mind mapping

making are too small and do not represent anything of major significance.

■ I draw a little cartoon face, with a questioning look, saying "Who cares?" I stare at the map and decide to draw a big circle around what is already drawn there and then work outside that circle to tap into the bigger picture.

■ In the overview area I draw a large eye. I think about the idea that if education requires conversation, it is very different from our old model in which the teacher talks while students listen, and the "no talking" among students rule is in effect most of the time. The key word I use is TRADITIONAL. Connected to the word I draw a teacher in the center with his or her "facts" being given to the students.

■ Below, I draw a classroom of students and teachers all involved in conversation. The key word that I decide to use here is EQUAL.

The notion of truth as a process makes me think that the teacher is not seen as the source of truth in this new model.

■ I add an arrow and the word TRUTH with Source branching from it to my teacher. A symbol that looks like a circled asterisk will represent truth for this map. I draw the same symbol above the heads of the conversing students as a cloud representing their conversations.

■ According to Palmer, the truth depends upon who "knows" it. The knowers, whether student or teacher, bring their own unique history to the learning and understanding processes. I draw another arrow from TRUTH to the students. The internal experience is an important element of each person's truth. As I think of this concept, I visualize a person with a truth symbol inside and a dotted line to the symbol outside.

■ I then draw a symbol of that person next to the key word, TRUTH. I can now stop and look at the map to see what it tells me and to gain new ideas.

This opportunity to stop and "learn from your map" is an important one. When you look at your own ideas represented graphically on paper, you can literally see what you are thinking — a process that enhances the internal conversation. That thought deserves a place on the map, too. I have just stumbled upon another relationship between mind mapping and Palmer's ideas.

From here the process could go anywhere. I could stop, satisfied that I have mapped the key ideas for now, continue with this map and see where it leads me, or make a new map. The new map could focus on one aspect of the old one with TRUTH represented in the central image. However, I would like to explore how these ideas can be put into everyday, practical application in the classroom. For that, a new map seems best, keeping the first one in view to give me ideas.

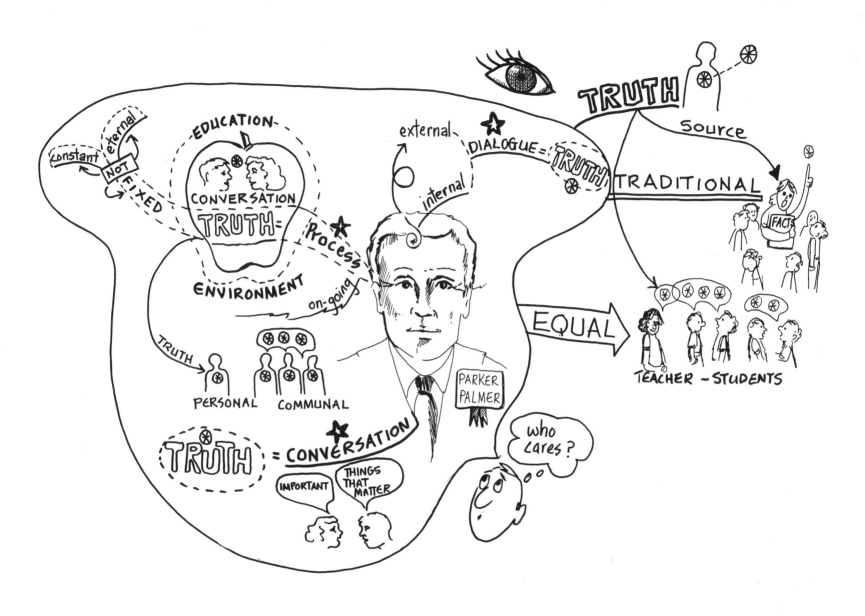

EDUCATION

constant
eternal
NOT
FIXED

CONVERSATION
TRUTH

★ Process

ENVIRONMENT

on-going

external

internal

DIALOGUE = TRUTH

TRUTH

Source

TRADITIONAL

FACT

EQUAL

TRUTH

TRUTH

PERSONAL   COMMUNAL

PARKER PALMER

TEACHER – STUDENTS

TRUTH = CONVERSATION ★

IMPORTANT

THINGS THAT MATTER

who cares?

★ = true of mind mapping

⊛ = TRUTH

111

The map on page 113 represents more ideas from Palmer.

For Your Students

As a result of making a new map, I generated the following ideas:

■ Ask students to write a story told from two points of view. This will help them discover that reality depends upon who is viewing it.

■ Create opportunities for students to teach each other and to teach the teacher. The child who draws well could show the class, step-by-step, how to create a specific mind map symbol.

■ Use cooperative learning groups to reinforce the conversation among students.

■ In an informal dialogue ask students and teachers to grade each other, thus reinforcing the concept of equality.

■ Assign cooperative learning groups in science, social studies, or history to find examples that show that what was once known as truth has since been completely revised.

■ Make mind maps on the topic of a controversial issue, asking everyone to take a slightly different point of view and map it.

■ Pose a question to the class and ask students to map their opinions in one color in the center of a large sheet of paper. Then collect, shuffle, and redistribute the maps. Ask students to use a different colored pen to add their response to the map, their agreement or disagreement, and the reasons why. Students can then take turns presenting the ways of knowing, both their contributions and those of the person who started the map.

■ Challenge your class to design a school based upon the equality principles of Parker Palmer. What would the schedule, class groupings, topics, and grading system look like in this new school?

■ Ask students to make a map that begins with what and who were most important to them when they were babies. After drawing a circle around that way of knowing, ask them to map the important things from their lives at different ages. As the map progresses, they will see how their worlds expanded from the time they were babies. A similar structure could be applied to the view of the planets from earth-centered or sun-centered.

The Outer Edge

In science, there is a concept called "edge of the map syndrome," which refers to the belief scientists have had, at various times through the ages. They have believed that they had discovered all there was to know about a certain subject: they had reached the edge of the map, and there was no more. Each time the edge was reached,

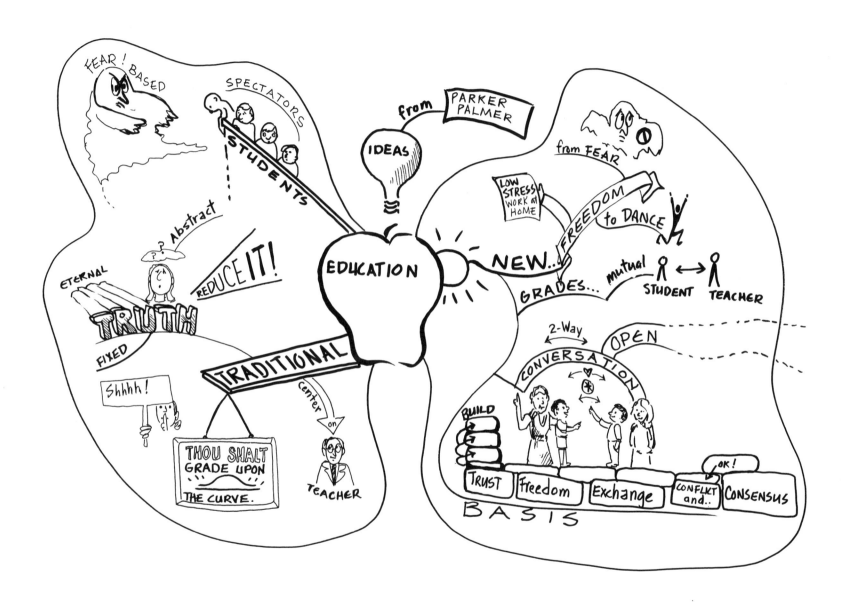

some foolhardy soul ventured off the map into unthought of territories and, naturally, stumbled into new information that made the old obsolete.

I like to borrow this concept when mind mapping. I often challenge students to a completed map and place it on a larger sheet of paper and go over the edge. This might require that they play with the notion that they are mapping the year 2010 or are recording the information as it might be seen by a visiting Martian. Social studies and history students can be challenged to create a map of "boundary breakers" such as Junko Tabei, the Wright brothers, Susan B. Anthony, Martin Luther King, and Christopher Columbus. The area beyond the known boundaries is rich with infinite possibilities, so why not explore and chart it?

As you can see on page 115, the guidelines for mind mapping, including one word per line, have been set aside in order to convey the concepts. This leads us to the form of recording ideas that breaks boundaries — mindscaping.

On pages 116 and 117, you will find two examples of mindscaping. An explanation of mindscaping begins on page 118.

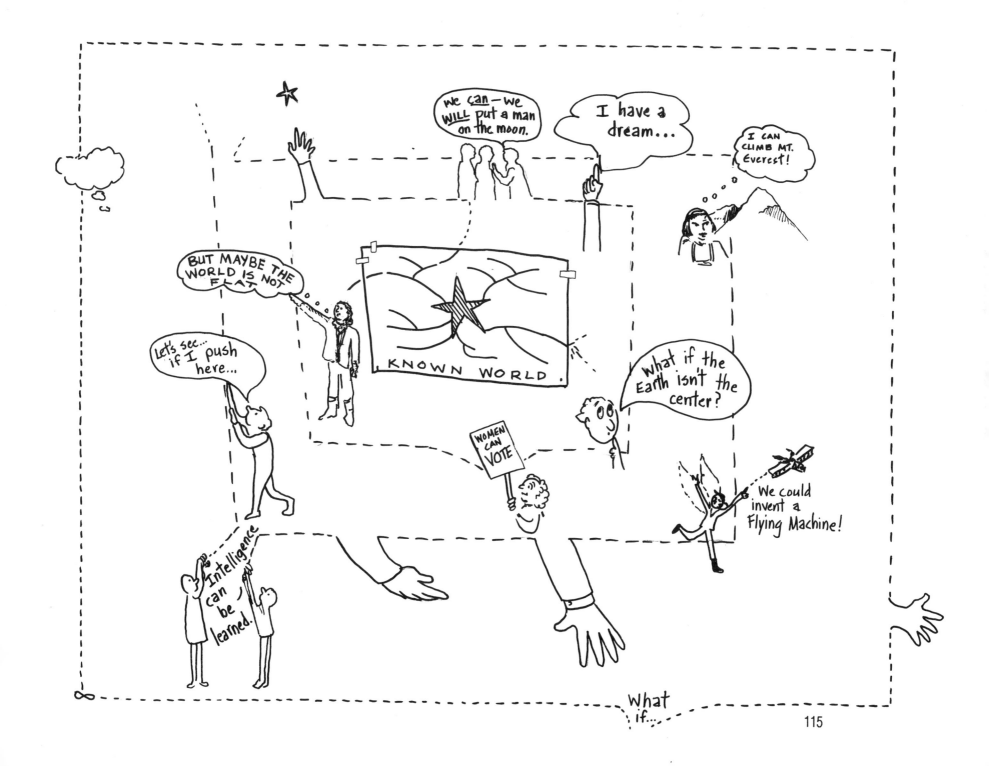

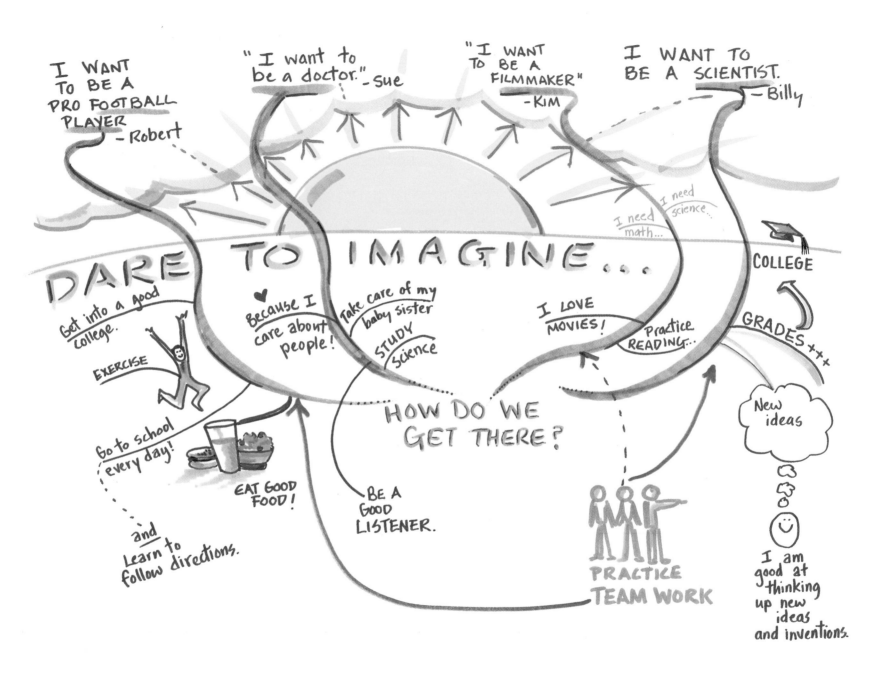

Kinesthetic Activities IDEAS

BE A CIRCLE!

MOVE IN A CIRCLE

ITS OK TO BE SILLY!

...mold your partner like CLAY

MOVING through math

6 people in a circle
LOOKING DOWN
How many can fit across? 2?
9 people in a circle... 3?
How many can fit across

All join in!
Group Shape
Give it a title

Don't break the glass!
Play "MIRROR"

Oh my gosh, Ive been drawn and quartered.

MOVE HALF of your body.

MOVE only 1/4 of your body.

SCIENCE ACT IT OUT
SOLID

AGENT
Substance MELTING
LIQUID

ITS A GAS!

117

Chapter 9

Mindscaping – A Variation

When I first learned to mind map, the rules served as important guidelines. I still find that for most purposes, such as daily planning, a mind map that adheres to the basic rules works wonderfully. Mind mapping is a system that encourages creativity and individuality, and soon I found myself moving away from the rules and creating maps that had no central image (gasp!), more than one word on a line, and other rebellious inventions. I discussed this with Tony Buzan, who understandably wanted me to present models of excellence in mind mapping whenever possible. We agreed that some of my creations were not examples of mind maps at all and needed to be given a new name.

The name I decided to use is MINDSCAPES. These landscapes of inner terrain are created with the following guidelines:

■ Anything goes. For example, you can make a mindscape that is mural sized and takes up an entire wall, or one that has little paper doors with messages behind them, or is written within segments of a geodesic dome.

■ Keep the mindscapes as varied as possible. In this way you are continually challenging yourself with finding new ways to put ideas on paper (or in computers or on T-shirts). The intuitive, holistic processing of your right hemisphere will remain engaged in the process more if it doesn't become too routine. Even your daily plan maps can look different every time you make one.

■ Begin the mindscape wherever you wish. Sometimes you may want to make a giant image on the page and fill it in with the your notes, ideas, and symbols. You might decide to put one idea on each half of the paper and compare or contrast them across the page. Perhaps you will make the mindscape resemble a jigsaw puzzle or a giant game board.

■ Use whatever resources are on hand. You might want to cut images from magazines to add to mindscapes, or use photographs for a mindscape about yourself or your family. Post-it notes, as I have mentioned, are great for not only adding new ideas, but changing them around to look at possible combinations.

■ Challenge yourself and your students. Give an award for the most unusual mindscape or for the most unusual idea presented. Ask provocative questions such as: Is it possible to weave two mindscapes together? Can several people work on one long mindscape at the same time? How can we use computers for mind maps or mindscapes?

■ For a challenging mindscape project, assign students the task of creating the mindscape of someone they are studying. What would the inner landscape of Benjamin Franklin, Leonardo daVinci, Cochise, Abraham Lincoln, Ernest Hemingway, Martin Luther King, Marie Antoinette, or Pee Wee Herman look like? What would be emphasized, what connections between ideas would they make? Which of their life experiences would show up in their inner landscapes? How did those experiences link to their later activities and accomplishments?

Comparisons and contrasts in mindscape form can be used to weigh decisions, analyze situations or current events, or look for similarities and differences.

■ For example, try a mindscape on the pluses, minuses, and interesting (or neutral) points of a possible action, event, or law. Mindscapes of this sort can assist students to look at a range of opinions and ideas before forming their own conclusions. The structure of the mindscape is flexible and allows you to set it up to serve you best — in sections, columns, overlapping shapes, or links in a chain.

The mindscape on page 116 was created during a brainstorming session with two-time U.S. Olympic Pentathlete Marilyn King, now of Beyond Sports in Oakland, California. She encourages children to dare to imagine goals for themselves and then brainstorm what they will need to do in order to move toward their goals.

King states, "If you can't imagine it, you can never do it. In my experience, the image always precedes the reality."

On page 117 you will find a mindscape that was created at a teachers' conference sponsored by New Horizons for Learning. The focus of the conference was "Living and Learning through the Many Intelligences."

Conclusion

The mindscape on the opposite page shows the path that will make learning exciting, challenging, and fun for teachers and students. Perhaps it is a path that you have already discovered — a path geared to the individual's unique style of learning.

You now have all the tools and information necessary to become a mind mapper and a mindscaper. The most valuable tool, of course, is your brain, with its unlimited potential. Next is your belief in the creative potential and imaginative powers that you and every one of your students possess. The guidelines and suggestions presented here are the beginning of a process that you can continue as you participate in the ultimate exploration — that of the human mind.

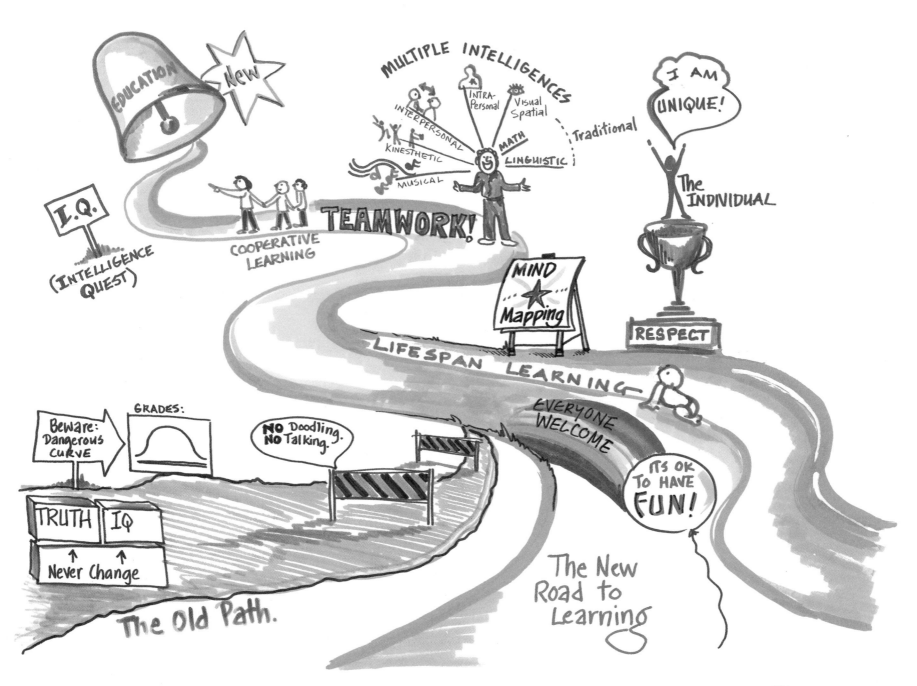

Bilbliography

Amery, Heather and Mila Reys. *The First Thousand Words in Spanish*. London: Usborne Publishing, 1988. (A great source for children to look up pictures of hundreds of items they might want to draw for mapping.)

Arnheim, Rudolf. *Art and Visual Perception*. Berkeley: University of California Press, 1954, 1974.

Barrett, Derm. "Intuition and Creative Thinking." *The Human Intelligence Newsletter*. 1989. (February-March):1-2

Botkin, James, Mahdi Elmandjra, and Mircea Malitza, *No Limits to Learning*. Elmsford, New York: Pergamon Press, 1979.

Brookes, Mona. *Drawing With Children*. Los Angeles: J. P. Tarcher, 1986. (To further the drawing skills of both children and adults; focus is on graphic design and cartoon elements of drawing.)

Buzan, Tony. *Use Both Sides of Your Brain*. New York: E.P. Dutton, 1974, revised and updated 1983.

Clark, Barbara. *Optimizing Learning*. Columbus, Ohio: Merrill Publishing Company, 1986.

Cousins, Norman. *Head First — The Biology of Hope*. New York: E. P. Dutton, 1989.

Covey, Stephen R. *The Seven Habits of Highly Effective People*. New York: Simon and Schuster, 1989.

Diamond, Marilyn. *Enriching Heredity*. New York: Free Press, 1988.

Dickinson, Dee. and Linda MacRae-Campbell. eds. *On The Beam, An International Human Resource Network*. Seattle: New Horizons for Learning, 1989. (This excellent newsletter will keep you up to date with innovative learning and cognitive research applied to education. Subscription information is available from New Horizons, 4649 Sunnyside North, Seattle, WA. 98103.)

Edwards, Betty. *Drawing on the Right Side of the Brain*. Los Angeles: J. P. Tarcher, 1989. (A wonderful lesson book that can really teach you to draw!)

————— *Drawing on the Artist Within*. New York: Simon & Schuster, 1987. (In this, her second book, Edwards explores self-understanding through art.)

Gelb, Michael. *Present Yourself*. Los Angeles: Jalmar Press, 1988. (Includes information on mind mapping and mind map summaries for every chapter. Available from High Performance Learning, 4613 Davenport Street NW, Washington DC, 20016.)

Gilman, Robert, ed. "In Context," *A Quarterly of Humane Sustainable Culture 18* (Winter 1988). (An excellent magazine that focuses on a different topic each issue.)

Goldberg, Elkhonon, and L.D.Costs. "Hemispheric Differences in the Aquisition of Descriptive Systems." *Brain and Language* 14 (1988): 144-173.

Gross, Ron. *Peak Learning*. Los Angeles: Audio Renaissance Tapes, Inc. 1988. Sound cassette.

Hermann, N. "The Creative Brain" *Training and Development Journal* 35 (1988): 10:10-16.

Houston, Jean. *The Possible Human*. Boston: J. P. Tarcher,1982.

——— *The Search for the Beloved*. Los Angeles: J. P. Tarcher, 1987.

Hughlings-Jackson, John. "On Aphasia and Kindred Affectations of Speech." *Brain*. XXXVIII (1915): 1-90.

Huxley, Aldous. *Island*. New York: Harper and Row, 1962.

Kline, Peter. *The Everyday Genius*. Arlington, VA: Great Ocean Publishers, 1988.

Margulies, Nancy and Michael Gelb. *The Mind Map*. Washington D.C. 1989. (Available from High Performance Learning 4613 Davenport Street NW 20016.)

Nicolaides, Kimon. *The Natural Way to Draw*. Boston: Houghton Mifflin Company, 1975.

Orcutt, David. *Worldsign Exposition*. Worldsign Communication Society, 1987. (Available from David Orcutt, Perry Siding, Winlaw, B.C. Canada, V0G2J0.)

Ornstein, Robert and Richard Thompson.*The Amazing Brain*. Boston: Houghton Mifflin, 1986.

Palmer, Parker. *To Know As We Are Known*. San Francisco: Harper and Row, 1983.

Restak, K. *The Brain: The Last Frontier*. New York: Doubleday, 1979.

Sacks, Oliver. *Seeing Voices — A Journey into the World of the Deaf*. Berkeley: University of California Press, 1989.

Samples, Bill. "Experiencing Your Experience." *Edges* 2 (June 1989)

Wenger, Win. *Toward a General Theory of Creativity and Genius*. Aurora, New York: United Educational Services. Available late 1990.

Bring master mind mapper Nancy Margulies into YOUR classroom with this 90-minute video

MAPS, MINDSCAPES, AND MORE

by Nancy Margulies, author of *Mapping Inner Space*

It's easy to learn and teach mind mapping when you see it demonstrated and applied in this exciting video. Watch master mind mapper Nancy Margulies teach her techniques to children and adults in a live demonstration, with one section especially for you to use in the classroom. The techniques shown here will take you beyond any previous books on mind mapping and include the newly developed Mindscape technique for graphic representation of your ideas.

Grades 4–Adult.
90-minute full-color video (VHS.)

ZV04 -A . . . $69